God, Secularization, and History

Essays in Memory of Ronald Gregor Smith

edited by
EUGENE THOMAS LONG

UNIVERSITY OF SOUTH CAROLINA PRESS
COLUMBIA, SOUTH CAROLINA

Library of Congress Cataloging in Publication Data

Main entry under title:

God, secularization, and history.

   CONTENTS: Long, E. T. God, secularization, and history.
—Ogden, S. M. Faith and secularity.—McKane, W. Tradition
as a theological concept. [etc.]
   1. Theology. 2. Smith, Ronald Gregor. 3. Smith,
Ronald Gregor—Bibliography. I. Long, Eugene Thomas, ed.
II. Smith, Ronald Gregor.
BR50.G545   201'.1   73-15712
ISBN 0-87249-293-1

In Memoriam
Ronald Gregor Smith
(1913–1968)

Preface

This volume, which is presented in memory of Ronald Gregor Smith, is the result of the advice and efforts of many persons, only a few of whom can be mentioned here. One can hardly think of Gregor Smith without thinking of his wife, Käthe Gregor Smith, and I can hardly think of this volume without thinking of the many ways in which she has assisted me. She cooperated with her husband on a number of occasions in translating significant works into the English language. And since his death she has worked tirelessly to continue to build the bridges of theological learning between Germany and the English-speaking world. I am indebted to her in particular for her assistance in the preparation of the bibliography and for her translations of Eberhard Bethge's essay, "Mündigkeit," and Helmut Gollwitzer's essay, "Thesen zum Verständnis der biblischen Rede von Gott."

Professor Gerhard Gloege of Bonn University, a long-standing friend of Gregor Smith, was preparing an essay for this volume when he became ill. With deep regret he wrote that he would be unable to complete his essay, "God and Secularization in F. M. Dostoevsky." I am grieved to report that since that time Professor Gloege has died.

Gregor Smith was close to many of the leading German philosophers and theologians of this century. He was indebted to their thought, but he also enjoyed and cherished his intimate acquaintances with them. Gregor Smith was a Scot by birth and a European at heart. If there was one theologian to whom he was most indebted both intellectually and personally it was Rudolf Bultmann. Gregor Smith was fond of saying that he was so indebted to the thoughts of

Bultmann that he was scarcely able to disentangle them from his own. Professor Bultmann celebrated his eighty-seventh birthday on August 20, 1971. In recent years he has not been in a position to write articles. However, I was delighted to receive from him the unsolicited communication which I have recorded below. It is a measure of Professor Bultmann's great spirit as well as his fondness and respect for Gregor Smith that he has done so.

I regret very much that I am unable to contribute an essay of my own to the *Festschrift* for Ronald Gregor Smith. But I should not want to fail to express my joy that his memory is being honored and appreciated in this way. For I can say that I am proud to have won his friendship through literary as well as personal communication. I took delight in his book *The New Man*, which convinced me that he and I shared much in our theological work and intentions, and I am most grateful that the arguments of this book were taken up and enriched by further significant essays in the posthumous volume, *The Free Man*. Here, his aim of expressing the traditional Christian confession in the language of modern men of all creeds has been impressively formulated. The subtitle of *The Free Man*, which is *Studies in Christian Anthropology*, also gives expression to one of Gregor Smith's essential concerns. For by "anthropology" he does not mean a dogmatic special doctrine. Anthropology means for him a reflection on the nature of man, a reflection which has universal theological interest and relates to all theological themes. Not only theologians but also many other readers who are asking about the meaning of human life today will welcome the recent publication of his work *The Doctrine of God*. This book is important not merely as a summary of his thought but above all because it further advances the work of his life. Here he develops thoughts to which he first gave expression in an address which he delivered in Marburg when the Theological Faculty of Marburg conferred upon him the honor of Doctor of Theology *honoris causa*.

Much of the initial work on this book was done during the year 1968–69 when I was a Research Fellow in the Duke University–University of North Carolina Cooperative Program in the Humanities, and I wish to express my appreciation for being given that opportunity. I am also grateful to the University of South Carolina Research and Productive Scholarship Fund for a grant which aided me in the preparation of the bibliography. The bibliography and the final editing of the manuscript were completed in Glasgow, where I resided at the home of Dr. and Mrs. Iain Nicol, and in Kiel-Kronshagen at the home of Mrs. Gregor Smith's sister, Frau Annelise Schulze-Rolfshörn. It gives me great pleasure to express my appreciation to these friends. Finally, I cannot fail to express my gratitude to Carolyn, Scott, and Kathryn, who forfeited a proper holiday in order that this volume be completed. To each of them I am more indebted than I could hope to say.

EUGENE THOMAS LONG
Columbia, South Carolina
May 1973

Contents

God,
Secularization, and
History

Introduction

The essays in this volume are presented as a tribute to the life and work of Ronald Gregor Smith. Contributors from among his many colleagues and students were invited to submit essays furthering discussion of the topic "God, Secularization, and History," which had occupied his attention for more than a decade. The selection of this topic has excluded many persons whose lives have been touched by him and who would have been able to contribute to a more general collection of essays. However, it seems appropriate that we should seek to continue the discussion to which he was so devoted even up to the time of his death.

Ronald Gregor Smith was born April 17, 1913, in Edinburgh, Scotland, to George Henry and Helen (Wilson Dea) Smith. In 1934 he graduated M.A. from the University of Edinburgh with first class honors in English language and literature. He received the B.D. degree with distinction in systematic theology from the same institution four years later. He continued his studies at the University of Munich, the University of Marburg, and the University of Copenhagen. In 1963 he was awarded the degree of Doctor of Divinity by the University of Edinburgh and the degree of Doctor of Theology *honoris causa* by the University of Marburg.

After serving as minister of the Lawson Memorial Church in Selkirk, Scotland (1939–44), Gregor Smith became a chaplain to the Scots Guards and in 1946 was appointed by the Control Commission for Germany as their Education Officer at Bonn University. On June 13, 1947, he was married to Katherina (Käthe) Elisabeth Helena Wittlake and in that same year he was appointed Associate Editor of the Student Christian Movement Press in London. Three years later he was made Managing Editor and Director, remaining in this capacity until 1956, when he was appointed Primarius Professor of Divinity at the University of Glasgow. In 1955 Gregor Smith delivered the Alexander Love Lectures at Ormond College, Melbourne. He delivered the F. D. Maurice Lectures for 1958 at King's College, London, and in 1964 he was appointed Visiting Professor of Theology at McCormick Theological Seminary in Chicago. In 1967 he was appointed Visiting Professor of Theology at Heidelberg University and was to have returned to the United States in 1969 as Visiting Professor of Theology at Colgate Rochester Divinity School and McCormick Theological Seminary and as Warfield Lecturer at Princeton Theological Seminary. Ronald Gregor Smith died on September 26, 1968, while returning to Glasgow from Germany.

Professor Gregor Smith, who gave much of his life toward building bridges of theological learning between Germany and the English-speaking world, was a person of considerable complexity. As a divinity student at Edinburgh he had translated Martin Buber's *Ich und Du*, and he looked continuously to twentieth-century Germany for philosophical and theological resources. Yet he was at home in the Enlightenment and a lover of the thought of David Hume. He was aptly described by the writer of the obituary in *The Times* as a Kierkegaardian figure, a person of gaiety and style whose life was touched with anguish. Yet he never lost the sense of community. He was an existentialist of sorts and was considered by many to be a radical theologian. Yet he never lost a concern for history and tradition and was critical of those who did.

It is this life which is reflected in the theological position he so persuasively expounded amidst the more orthodox setting of established theology in Scotland. As editor, teacher, and writer he worked to break the bonds of insularity and to introduce the provocative and exacting character of European scholarship into British theological discussions. And, as one writer has commented, it is to his lasting credit that he was able to do so with such literary elegance and conciseness of expression.

The central theme of this collection of essays is "God, Secularization, and History," and the first chapter by Eugene Long introduces this theme and Gregor Smith's contribution to it. Discussions of the idea of God cannot, without serious consequences, ignore the secular view of reality which has come to dominate Western culture since the Renaissance. Yet many of the traditional theological categories are unable to carry the burden of speaking of God in a manner that has meaning for secular man. There have been, of course, a number of attempts to face up to this dilemma. But in many cases these efforts have led in the direction of an uncritical appropriation of dogmatic secularism and a failure to speak significantly of God. It is here that Gregor Smith's work gains its importance, for while he has argued forcefully that the world at which the theologian and the secularist look are one and the same he has also argued that theologians must learn to speak meaningfully of the transcendence of God within this world.

Gregor Smith has made clear his belief that the options for the Christian believer are not limited to those of classical theism and reductionist secularism. He proposes understanding the Christian faith in the context of history, history qualified by the event of Christ in which God's transcendence is understood as a historical transcendence. Here he finds the possibility for an authentic or Christian secularity. Schubert Ogden speaks on this topic in the second chapter of this book. Ogden argues that although the exact relation between Christian faith in God and secularity is *the* problem of contemporary theology, it is insoluble until we expose and reject the oversimplification of this problem which is implicit in two commonly accepted assumptions—that one can be truly secular only by accepting some version of modern secularism and that one can be religious only by accepting the claims of classical theism.

Secularism, according to Ogden, denies that anything beyond life in this world is significant, and classical theism denies that the world is fully significant. But in neither case are these denials entailed in the more positive affirmations of secularity and Christian faith in God. Therefore, once these common assumptions are exposed as baseless oversimplifications, the problem of faith and secularity becomes a new one in which one is again able to ask whether it is not possible to be fully secular and yet affirm what is positive in classical theism.

Sensitive readers of Gregor Smith's works have noted that his view of man as thoroughly human and secular was inseparably related to his understanding of man within the context of historical tradition. Indeed, one of his major criticisms of much contemporary writing on the idea of God was that the writers lacked the context of the tradition out of which their essays came. Yet his recognition of the significance of tradition did not result in enslavement to it. The historical tradition was not authoritative for Gregor Smith, but it was one of the partners in the dialogue between presentness and pastness, and he considered this dialogue essential to a genuinely secular existence. It is fitting that William McKane, whose work was cited in this context in Gregor Smith's last book, has chosen to write on the topic "Tradition as a Theological Concept." McKane argues that the issues raised by Gregor Smith are also at the center of the Old Testament debate, that Old Testament scholars must turn from the viewpoint which accents the religious ideas of the Old Testament as theologically or ethically normative and turn toward a view which sees them as part of a creative process in which they take on significance only in relation to the changing context in which the life of faith responds to them.

In Chapter 4, "Theology: Art or Science?," Harry Wardlaw explores the implications of this connection between faith and history for theological method. Agreeing with Gregor Smith that theology begins with the question *Whence do we receive?*, Wardlaw seeks to answer this question by exposing the historical roots of faith. Since faith is grounded in a living historical context, theology cannot, without error, make God into an object of scientific understanding. Theology must, rather, unfold within a historical dialogue between the theologian and the living faith of the persons and communities of faith. The important thing, therefore, is not that the theologian agree with the decrees of the apostles, church fathers, and reformers, but that he participate in a genuine living dialogue with them.

Just how the past is present to the contemporary man of faith is the focal point for Iain Nicol's essay, "History and Transcendence." Attempting to extend Gregor Smith's suggestion that the transcendent confronts us from out of the past in making a claim upon our present existence, Nicol argues that the past is not present as a solid and secure aggregate of facts about it but as an address. In the living connection of the past with the present the meaning of these events is said to be apperceived as being compresent to and with the person addressed.

The implications of a more dynamic view of history for a definition of the Christian kerygma are explored by Douglas Templeton. As he views it, the problem in defining kerygma is to avoid on the one hand the tendency to reduce it to a set of timeless truths and on the other hand the tendency to lose its grounding in particular historical events. By means of the doctrine of the "paradoxical identity" of the activities of man and the activities of God, Templeton argues that kerygma is words spoken by Christians, i.e., by persons whose existence is qualified by the existence of Jesus of Nazareth in such a way that they are made free and responsible for others. More precisely, the Christian is qualified by those who have been thus qualified. And as what Jesus said and did was paradoxically what God said and did, so the Christian's talk of relation to Jesus, if led by the Spirit, is at the same time talk of God. The doctrine of paradoxical identity applies now as well as then.

Gregor Smith was fond of saying, "We have to do with God in history and nowhere else." And this implied for him that in speaking of God it was essential to move beyond both mythological and classical attempts to speak of God. He proposed to speak of God only in the context of God's being for man in history. The seventh and eighth chapters of this volume focus on this theme. In speaking of the transcendence of God as analogous to or coincident with the transcendent element within personal relations, A. D. Galloway seeks to avoid the existentialist tendency to identify knowledge and love of God with self-understanding and the tendency of some secular theologians to identify it with knowledge and love of neighbor. The attaining of any new level in self-understanding and in knowing and loving our neighbor is said to be coincident with the attaining of a new level in knowing and loving God. God in Christ determines the context within which men are persons, and in this context God is known and spoken of.

In a somewhat related way, Helmut Gollwitzer also maintains that God's being-for-us must be spoken of in the language of per-

sonal relations. This is said to exclude an impersonal, metaphysica
speaking of God removed from the contingent historical situatio
in which we are adjudged and a claim is laid upon us. Yet speech i
not about God conceived as a kind of enlarged man ruling the earth
Biblical speech about God is not speech about God's being-is
himself but speech about the historical forms in which God's ac
dress is heard and speech about our own hearing of this address
Biblical speech refers to the "voice of God," God's confronting u
in historical forms that lay a claim upon us. And faith is the hearin
of this "voice" and the letting it penetrate our lives again and agair

The exact nature of this life is the theme of the concludin
chapter by Eberhard Bethge. According to Bethge, the process o
secularization and the self-liberation of man from ecclesiastica
guardianship has made it impossible for the Church to define th
Christian life in terms of obedience to some norms alien to that life
The Church, rather, must release the individuals for their maturity
their being of age. And this being of age is defined in relation t
Christ. In this relation, and thus in recognition of his own limits an
possibilities, man is set free. He comes of age. Because, however, it i
freedom which acknowledges man's limits and possibilities, it i
therefore never unlimited licentiousness of the kind that restrict
the freedom of others. On the contrary, it is a being free which ac
knowledges its own givenness and enables others to gain power ove
their own lives.

I

God, Secularization, and History

Eugene Thomas Long
University of South Carolina

One hesitates today to use the word "secularization" because of its tendency to evoke uncritical responses of praise or disgust. Yet it is the case that secularization as a social process and as a way of viewing reality is a dominant factor in Western culture. Whether secularization be understood to have its origin in the Judaeo-Christian tradition, in reaction to it, or even prior to it, it has been a prominent fact in Western culture since the Renaissance, and discussion of the meaning of "God" can ignore it only with serious consequences.

Secularization means above all a temporal, this-worldly view of reality, a concern with the world in which man lives and makes his own being and a rejection of a dualistic view of reality with its other world of timeless truths. In the secular view man accepts responsibility for his own selfhood and refuses to surrender that responsibility to an alien authority whether it be church, state, or God. Secularization may, but need not, mean the affirmation of a kind of arbitrary freedom which breaks off from all sense of community. It does mean a concentration on the temporal or historical existence of man and a break with those views of man which would deny him responsibility for his existence in the world.

In some cases secularization results in affirmation of man's freedom and a simple and undialectical rejection of faith in God. In this case God may be understood as the Wholly Other who can be reached only by a rejection of man's free existence in the world and a religious flight into the beyond. However, many theologians have argued that belief in God is consistent with the process of secularization. In fact, it is occasionally argued that the secular view of reality

9

has its foundation in the Christian faith.[1] While this may be an oversimplification of a very complex phenomenon, it is surely the case that the Christian faith, as understood in contemporary theology, is not merely antithetical to the process of secularization and its view of reality. Theism has long since abandoned the mythological view of God as an object capable of being perceived by one or more of the senses. But contemporary theologians and philosophers of religion have also challenged the traditional theistic view of God as an object transcendent to the world, the personal yet intangible creator who governs the world in some mysterious way. It is argued that the Judaeo-Christian tradition itself gives man reason for a more temporal view of God in which man is able to get along in the world without a transcendent benevolent deity who keeps things on course, fills in the gaps in our knowledge, and occasionally intervenes in the course of life.

It is, of course, one thing to say that faith in God and secularization are not antithetical or that the Judaeo-Christian tradition gives man a basis for a more temporal or secular view of God; it is another thing actually to speak of God in this sense. Some theologians seem simply to have given up any serious effort to speak of God in a meaningful sense. For instance, Paul van Buren seems to have equated secularity with a positivistic view of reality and thus concludes "The empiricist in us finds the heart of the difficulty not in what is said about God, but in the very talking about God at all. We do not know 'what' God is, and we cannot understand how the word 'God' is being used."[2] What was traditionally referred to as the transcendence of God seems to be replaced by what van Buren refers to as the contagion of Jesus' freedom. The irony of this situation is that while such views may seem at first glance to gain more acceptance

[1] Many persons have argued that the Christian view of the world and God provided the basis for the contemporary scientific and secular view of reality. See for example: M. B. Foster, "The Christian Doctrine of Creation and the Rise of Modern Science," *Mind* XLII (1934); Friedrich Gogarten, *Verhängnis und Hoffnung der Neuzeit* (Stuttgart: Friedrich Vorwerk Verlag, 1953); and C. F von Weizsäcker, *The Relevance of Science* (New York: Harper, 1964), pp 106–107, 162–164. For a somewhat different analysis see Martin Heidegger "Die Zeit des Weltbildes," *Holzwege* (Frankfurt: Vittorio Klostermann, 1963)

[2] Paul van Buren, *The Secular Meaning of the Gospel* (London: S.C.M Press, 1963), pp. 84, 141 ff.

om secularists, the word "God" seems to take on no more signif-
ance than it does in the writing of those theologians who merely
ject the process of secularization and abandon the task of speaking
f God in the context of the secular view of reality.

More promising attempts to speak of God have sought to express
critical and dialectical relationship between talk of God and the
rocess of secularization. In these cases the theologian abandons
either his task of speaking of God in the context of the world nor
is role as critic of those excesses of secularization which result in an
rbitrary and closed view of reality and perhaps in a loss of man's
utonomy and responsibility. In the English-speaking world it is
robably Ronald Gregor Smith who has been most articulate in
xpressing the need for this dialectical understanding of the relation
etween Christian faith in God and the secular view of reality.

Theology and Secularity

The central fact which lies behind many of Gregor Smith's efforts
his own deep concern for the division between Church and society
hich became prominent in Western civilization following the Ren-
issance. Western civilization, ignoring for the most part its roots
the Judaeo-Christian tradition, asserted the autonomy of human
fe which understood itself from within its own history. The
Church, failing to see the continuity between the emergence of au-
nomous human life and the Christian faith, sought refuge in a
ew heteronomous or alien structure of creed and doctrine which
ould replace the broken tradition of the medieval Church. This
ffort to assert a controlling authority over the world is understood
y Gregor Smith to have manifested itself in recent years in dialec-
cal theology or the theology of the Word. While Gregor Smith
oes not reject the many valuable insights of this theology, he is
ritical of its tendency to isolate itself and hence the Word of God
om the world in which men live.

This often sharp and violent divergence between the Church and
e world or between theology and the world has resulted in a sit-
ation, according to Gregor Smith, in which neither the life of au-
nomous secularized man nor the heteronomous life of the Church

is capable of being fulfilled. Separated from its roots in the Word
of God, the autonomous life of man runs into the contradiction
that freedom becomes the victim of ideologies which compete for
the control of man. And the heteronomous life of the Church, separated from the life of man, removes the Word of God from the
life of man by putting it into the dimension of a meaningless wholly
other.

The way of theology beyond this apparent impasse cannot then
come by way of the imposition of some heteronomous theology onto
the picture of modern man. Theology cannot be the mere elabora-
tion of propositions or doctrines about God, nor the maintenance
of some specific world view over against some other secular ideology.
Such efforts are subject to the same limits as the various secular
ideologies such as Marxism and scientism; that is, they deny the
freedom and autonomy of man to decide his own life in the world.
Theology must begin not in some world removed from the life of
secular man but in that very world which is shared by all men, i.e.,
the secular world. Theology has its beginning in this world alongside other human undertakings rather than with the Word of God
removed from this world.

Gregor Smith gave expression to this approach to theology in 1959
at a conference on "The Meaning of the Secular" at the Ecumenical
Institute in Bossey, Switzerland, when he said, "I consider myself
to be simultaneously some kind of theologian and immersed willy
nilly in the secular styles of apprehension and living. . . . My fundamental assumption is that the world which the theologian looks at
and the world which the secularist looks at are one and the same."
He is suggesting here that although he, as a theologian, speaks out
of the experience of a particular historical tradition, he does not intend to appeal to revelatory events outside the general experience
of man. On the contrary, he is saying that he shares with all men a
common secular experience from within which the historical revelation of the Christian faith has to be received and comprehended.
Theology must then make its beginnings in the very ambiguities of
the empirical historical situation of man.[3]

In approaching theology in this manner Gregor Smith gives

[3] Ronald Gregor Smith, *The Free Man* (London: Collins, 1969), pp. 24, 45.

credence to the responsibility of the theologian for speaking to his own world. Yet he does so without contradicting the theologian's responsibility of speaking of God. It is possible, of course, for a theologian to arrive at a point in which he no longer believes himself able to speak of God in a meaningful sense, and honesty demands that he then cease doing so. However, to the extent that he professes to be a theologian he must continue to speak of God. This is not to say that he is bound to any particular metaphysical idea of God. It is simply to say that it would be very strange, if not contradictory, to fail to speak of God, for theology itself means God-talk. In this Gregor Smith differs from the so-called death of God theologians. He believes them to be right in pointing to the malaise of our time and in rejecting the God of classical theism. But he seeks to preserve what he considers to be an unsurrenderable element in what has been traditionally called the transcendence of God. God's transcendence is for Gregor Smith a historical transcendence, God's history with man, and this he sees to be basic to a full understanding of the secular mode of life.

It is then secularity, or the secular understanding of life, which provides the common ground between the theologian and the secularist. The theologian speaks of God. Yet he speaks of him from within a shared secularity, a shared view of humanity. If God is then to have any significance it must be possible to show that this secularity in some sense points to or is dependent on God. At this point I would wish to argue for the need of a natural or philosophical theology. That is, unless one takes the view that theology appeals to some unique occasion discontinuous with ordinary experience and philosophical understanding, one ought to be able to show some context within ordinary experience in relation to which the word "God" can be shown to be meaningful.

Because of his concern to give adequate expression to the historicity of God, Gregor Smith was reluctant to follow in the direction of natural or philosophical theology in any ordinary sense. However, he does not simply follow the Barthians in denying all connections between the theological and philosophical uses of the word "God." He proposes, rather, a new approach to natural theology which he says is "empirical, historical, positivist ('He that hath seen me hath seen the Father'), grounded in the Word."[4] As I under stand it, a natural theology which is developed along these line would be such only in some qualified sense. Gregor Smith says tha it is natural theology which must be at the same time *fides quaeren intellectum*, a theology which acknowledges that there can be n God-talk, that is, no positive description of God, apart from fait

Gregor Smith is proposing an alternative other than that of a objectifying metaphysics or an immanentist process theory of hi tory. And although all of the details are not worked out, it can b said that it is a natural theology rooted in a radical assessment o man's historicity. In every historical encounter there is said to be residue, a mystery which is not capable of being explained by trad tional frames of thought. Starting with man, we discover that ma is ultimately a question to himself which admits of no answer out o man's creative rationality. Man is not primarily a doer but a receive of the reality which is possible in each encounter. This reality come by way of the other whom he encounters, yet it is neither himse nor the other. As such, we participate in it and are permitted t point to it as that which summons and addresses us.

As I understand it, this does not eliminate all talk of God outsid the actual encounter of faith. But it does suggest that such talk is a best a negative talk of God or, better perhaps, talk of man's finit ness and limitedness. This is implicit in Gregor Smith's analysis o secularism to which we must now turn. As an aid to understandin this analysis of the process of secularization attention should b called to the distinction which is sometimes made between th process of secularization and the corruption of that process. On might speak of an authentic and inauthentic secularization. Th ologians at times make a related distinction between secularity an secularism or between Christian secularity and secularism. Withou engaging in a detailed discussion of the implications of such di tinctions I want to call attention to the fact that we can distinguis between a temporal view of reality in which man's autonomy an responsibility are recognized and an abortion of that view, a redu

[4] Ronald Gregor Smith, *The Doctrine of God* (London: Collins and Phil delphia: Westminster, 1970), pp. 174, 145 ff.

ionist or positivistic view of reality which, ironically, results in a
oss of freedom and individuality when technology comes to control
he life of man as well as the natural resources.

When Gregor Smith tells us that as a theologian he claims no special authority from any unexamined revealed truths, that he simply
wishes to observe phenomena, and that he begins from within the
ambiguities of the historical situation, he means that he begins
alongside others in a situation where the process of secularization
has been aborted. Thus, he argues that the problem of secularism is
not its basic assumption, namely, that man is solely responsible for
his own history. The problem is, rather, that there is a basic contradiction in the contemporary secularized style of life in that freedom
has been replaced by bondage and personal responsibility by impersonal existence. The inadequacy of the secularist point of view is
then not to be found in its concentration on man and his history but
in its failure to concentrate enough on them. Secularism is not secularist enough, and the result is that man's freedom is subordinated
o some alien world view.

Freedom, unless it is simply accidental or arbitrary (in which case
t would not be freedom), lives in accordance with some norm or
criterion. But just because of this there is always the risk that freedom will be replaced by bondage to that norm. And this, according
o Gregor Smith, is just what happens when man seeks to secure his
freedom through bondage to some world view such as scientism,
relativism, Marxism, or even Christendom. Man loses the very thing
which he is seeking to secure. What is called for, then, is a critique
of all ideologies or world views, a demonstration of their impotence
o secure man's freedom and responsibility. Just as dread or anxiety
in existential philosophy calls into question those finite meanings
which lay claim on our lives, thereby freeing us from them and
throwing us back upon ourselves, so the analysis of secularism, the
showing of its limits and contradictions, frees us from those ideologies which contradict man's autonomy and opens him up to
new possibilities of self-understanding. Gregor Smith seeks a radical or authentic secularity and this "is reached only when the
secularist process or movement goes to the very end of the road.

Freed of all ideologies, in complete freedom man is then left entirely by himself."[5]

As we shall see, this analysis of secularism does not in and of itself provide the ultimate basis for the realization of freedom. Such is said to be realized only in the decision of faith. However, implicit in this analysis is the suggestion that human existence, in its failure to secure freedom in rational or empirical terms, points us into the dimension in which this freedom is realized as a gift arising out of the encounter with historical transcendence. At the end of the road, says Gregor Smith, when man is freed of all ideologies, when he is left entirely by himself, he faces the question of his existence in a new and radical way which may open him up to a new apprehension of himself and his world. The question of the meaning of human existence as free remains. Only now, the answers assigned to this question by the world have been challenged. In this situation man is faced with a decision which is reflected in his asking, "Is the controlling power in human life made by men or not?" To answer no to this question, as does Gregor Smith, reflects a decision, but one which is not simply arbitrary, for it has already been suggested that answering yes results in a contradiction in which one's freedom is lost. To call into question the meanings given to the world by man is surely to call man into question. And yet meaning remains at least in man's continuing to question the meaning of his essential being. But what then is the source of this meaning? Whence does it come?

According to Gregor Smith, it comes as a gift from within history. The question *Who am I?* has its answer in another question: *Adam, where art thou?* This question is addressed to man from within history, in the encounter with the message concerning Jesus as the Christ. Gregor Smith modifies Tillich's suggestion that man's efforts to solve the riddle of his own being and destiny are shown fruitless by Jesus, who came to destroy religion. Man's efforts are not merely destroyed so as to erase all hope, but, rather, by emptying the world of hope, the nevertheless of faith comes into its own. In the face of

[5] *Free Man*, p. 41, 137 ff.; Ronald Gregor Smith, *Secular Christianity* (London: Collins, 1966), p. 172.

he inadequacy of his religious yearnings or theological enterprises,
nan meets God's Word, God's address for him.

This Word, which is spoken to man from within history, is a
iberating Word which does not remove man from the world but
rees him for it. Freedom in this sense is realized in choosing to live
rom beyond the limits of the finite. It is a choosing and a being
esponsible which comes as a gift of transcendence, a deciding for
hat selfhood which is not limited by the world but is open to it. The
vorld is negated only in the sense that it is no longer self-enclosed,
10 longer the destroyer of human autonomy. In faith, man is re-
eased from bondage to the world only to be put back into it as the
ime and place of human responsibility.[6]

It is clear from what has been said that theology as Gregor Smith
inderstands it is a hermeneutical undertaking. It seeks to under-
tand or interpret. Yet this task does not take its beginning in a
radition alien to secular culture. On the contrary, it begins in the
ecular world where all men are. This beginning is made possible by
he fact that the process of the secularization or historization of
1uman existence is understood to be grounded in the encounter
vith God in Christ. Thus, an authentic understanding of secularity
s at the same time an understanding of the Christian faith. To say,
hen, that theology begins in the secular world where all men are is
1ot to say that it is isolated from the past. On the contrary, Gregor
imith sees hermeneutics as a way of understanding ourselves in
elation to the past. However, this past is not merely a set of data
vhich is brought forth to fill up the empty vessel of the present.
"Rather this present situation is, for each one of us, one in which
ve are already embedded . . . in the structures of tradition. . . . Mod-
rn hermeneutics is the unity, in language, of past events with pres-
nt decisions. Thus I do not, in the process of understanding, simply
onceptualize the past: but I respond to the truth which I meet in
ach new hermeneutical situation."[7]

The basic question for theology, says Gregor Smith, is not *what*

---

[6] *Free Man*, pp. 38 ff., 53 ff.; *Secular Christianity*, pp. 39 ff., 155–156;
)octrine of God, pp. 123 ff.

[7] *Doctrine of God*, pp. 31–32. There are a number of parallels between Go-

are we to do? or *how are we to think of things?* but *whence do we receive?* And in answering this question with words such as "grace" or "otherness," the theologian may be said to be engaging in a kind of witnessing or pointing to that which can never be possessed in a system of thought about God and the world. Theology, thus, begins not with the dogmatic tradition of the Church but with the human condition as such. Yet this beginning points ultimately to an understanding of and dialogue with the Judaeo-Christian tradition, which is a part of the cultural condition of man. Now the biblical and ecclesiastical traditions are seen in a living historical perspective rather than as isolated dogmatic traditions. And theology is not a dogmatic statement concerning God and his attributes but a recounting of the engagement of God with men in their own history. Theology, then, may be said to reflect on God in the context of historical action and thus to witness to the historicity of God.[8]

The Historicity of God

Gregor Smith's contemplation of the meaning of the secular leads him to reject the classical idea of God as a timeless, wholly other being. He even shares something of van Buren's more radical approach to the problem. He certainly agrees with Van Buren and the whole tradition of negative theology which maintains that we must be silent about God as he is in himself. He also seems to agree with van Buren when the latter says: "The language of faith, by referring to a transcendent element, indicates that something has happened to the believer, rather than that he has done something."[9] However, he makes it clear that he diverges sharply from van Buren when the latter moves beyond this to the reduction of the transcendence of God to the level of empirical verification and hence to a view which finds no meaning in the expression "transcendence of God." Ac-

---

garten's and Gregor Smith's understanding of the secular. Gregor Smith notes that it is Gogarten who has made the most elaborate and direct contribution to the theme of secular Christianity. See *Secular Christianity*, pp. 151 ff., and *Free Man*, pp. 83 ff., 137 ff.

[8] *Free Man*, pp. 28 ff., 50 ff.; *Doctrine of God*, pp. 21 ff.

[9] van Buren, *op. cit.*, p. 141. Cf. *Secular Christianity*, p. 189.

rding to Gregor Smith, we must speak not only of Jesus and the
ntagion of his freedom but also of the transcendence of God
hich encounters us in Jesus.

It is clear that Gregor Smith's thought cannot, without error, be
o closely aligned with some of the more widely known versions of
cular theology or death of God theology. He conceives his primary
sk to be that of speaking of the transcendence of God in a way that
 consistent with his own secular view of reality. If on the one hand
ne ignores transcendence and hence the ontological difference be-
veen God and man, one runs the risk of identifying God with some
imension of the world, thereby inheriting all the problems asso-
ated with entirely naturalistic and solipsistic views of the world,
icluding the loss of freedom, which is fundamental to genuine
cularity. If on the other hand one opts for that traditional theolog-
al view in which God is understood as wholly other Being, one puts
ieself in the position of accepting a dualism between the world of
od and the world of phenomena, and once this dualism is posited
ere is no way of thinking the two worlds together again.

If, then, we are to be able to bridge the gap between the secular
d religious worlds, the transcendence of God must in some sense
e immanent. For Gregor Smith, this means talking of God's his-
ricity, God's being-for-us in history. Transcendence in this view
nnot be a timeless supra-historical reality but is itself a dimension
ithin history. It is the event of otherness which presses in upon
an, calling him into question and laying a claim upon him. The
anscendence of God is thus understood in a way analogous to the
ay in which we understand the transcendence of another person to
. This event is not simply and directly observable. It is hidden ex-
pt to the eye of faith. Yet this is not to say that ordinary explana-
ons are set aside or replaced by faith. Faith, rather, is a response to
 address from within history which recognizes the presence of
od within it, simultaneous with its everyday meaning. God is
iown only as he gives himself to us in history, a givenness which we
uld not create or imagine but can only receive.[10]

In some ways, Gregor Smith stands quite near to Martin Buber in

[10] *Secular Christianity*, p. 122; see also pp. 21, 41 ff. and *Free Man*, pp.
—23, 129–30.

his understanding of God. Both agree that man's co-humanity is no
exhausted by an analysis of the confrontation of one person with
another person. The genuine relation between persons, rather
points beyond itself to a realm between man and man, the realm o
the spirit, whose gift of grace and responsibility grants the relation
between persons. Buber has reference to this realm of spirit between
persons when he says that in every I-Thou relation we catch
glimpse of the eternal Thou. And Gregor Smith speaks in a similar
manner when he says, "to describe him [God] means either that we
say nothing or that we say he is nothing. But this *nihil* is not the or
phaned horror of Jean Paul's vision in *Siebenkas*, nor the flagran
defiance of Nietzsche's challenge. But it is the *nihil* of the *Ungrun*
which is simply the intensification, by analogy, of the mystery of al
human existence and all human interrelation. Co-humanity carrie
with it the unavoidable historical reality of the inter-humanity an
inter-humanity points unavoidably to the reality of God, as with u
for us, in us, and yet not of us."[11]

If, however, Gregor Smith can be understood to stand near Bube
at this point, he stresses that he wishes to avoid the tendency o
Buber to empty faith of its essential historicity. And this, he say
can be avoided only by making clear the historicity of encounte
The Christian faith has to do with the transcendence of God i
history. God's transcendence is encountered in the proclamation
concerning Jesus as a disturbance or a demand addressed to ou
being. And faith is "the way in which we acknowledge the presenc
of a claim upon our life rising up out of the past. This past is the pas
of Jesus, as presented to us in the message concerning him."[1]
Christian faith may be said to be related both to the past and to th
future. The events of the past make demands or claims upon th
present through the proclamation of the Christian faith, and th

[11] *Free Man*, p. 154.
[12] *Secular Christianity*, pp. 191–192. Gregor Smith's understanding of th
relation between faith and history is much indebted to Bultmann. See, for e
ample, R. G. Smith, *The New Man* (London: S.C.M. Press, 1956), pp. 85 ff
where he indicates that Bultmann provides the basis for an understanding o
transcendence as historical. However, Gregor Smith was anxious to make mor
explicit the dialectical understanding of the relation between faith and histor
than Bultmann does. For his critique of Buber and his similar critique of Joh
Baillie, see *Whole Man*, pp. 17–19, and *Doctrine of God*, pp. 126 ff.

orms the basis for the believer's decision concerning the future. The
Christian faith, then, is a historical faith, in that it arises as the consequence of certain events in history, and these events constitute the
shape and content of faith.

To the extent that this faith involves a knowing, it is other than
the result of discursive reasoning or a projection of self-understanding. It is, rather, the acknowledging of the presence of a claim upon
our lives rising out of the past, the past of Jesus as presented to us in
the message concerning him. Faith is a decision concerning our
being in which we acknowledge the controlling power in our life to
come from beyond ourselves. Yet this affirmation of God, according
to Gregor Smith, is inseparable from the message concerning Jesus,
in the face of which the decision is made. "We cannot at this point
as it were cast off into the sea of God's being: there is no being of
God for us other than his being-for-us in Christ. But this is his reality. He is constantly himself, and is never other than he is in
Christ." [13]

The Bible, according to Gregor Smith, recounts this engagement
of God with men in their history, the engagement which speaks of
a demand laid upon people in the actual historical possibilities
of their time. In this way, the writers of the Bible are said to bear
witness to the historicity of God, to his "coming to speech" within
a situation of personal encounter in which a demand is laid upon a
people and responded to in faith or unbelief.[14] However, it is not
mere demand to which faith responds and the Bible witnesses. It
is at the same time a gift of forgiveness or liberation, which sets men
free to respond to the demand. And it is here, in the paradox of faith
as a free response to the claim of God upon man, that Gregor Smith
finds the basis for his understanding of a radical or Christian
secularity.

[13] *Secular Christianity*, p. 192.
[14] *Free Man*, pp. 50 ff.; *Secular Christianity*, pp. 26 ff., 117 ff. The phrase
"coming to speech" is intended to emphasize the revelatory event as a public
event and has the meaning of laying a demand on a people through actual
historical situations. In *Doctrine of God*, p. 32. Gregor Smith draws a parallel to
Ernst Fuchs' use of the term "speech-event." However, the use of this term can
also be traced to Hamann. See Gregor Smith's essay, "The Living and Speaking
God," *Hibbert Journal* XLII (April 1944), and *J. G. Hamann, A Study in Christian Existence* (London: Collins, 1960), pp. 64 ff.

In the crucifixion of Jesus, the story of Israel reaches a point i
which man is liberated from all powers that keep him in bondag
In Jesus' cry of dereliction from the cross, the world is believed to b
cleared of all gods, i.e., of all ideologies, powers, and hopes. Th
faiths of secularism which seek to build up assurances within th
world and to secure man from the ultimacy of the question of th
meaning of human existence are put to an end. Man is released fror
these powers, and in this clearing the Christian faith has its realit
Faith in this sense is not belief in some world view or idea of Go
but the receiving of forgiveness in Christ, which frees man fror
bondage to the world and simultaneously makes him responsible fc
it. Thus, the relation of faith to the world is a dialectical one. Ma
is released from the world which controls him but put back into it a
the place of his responsibility. Thus, Gregor Smith seems to ech
Bonhoeffer's saying, "In Christ we are offered the possibility of pa
taking in the reality of God and in the reality of the world, but nc
in the one without the other. The reality of God discloses itself onl
by setting me entirely in the reality of the world, and when I er
counter the reality of the world, it is always already sustained, ac
cepted and reconciled in the reality of God."[15]

The transcendence of God, then, is a historical transcendence i
that faith encounters in history God's being-for-us in the messag
concerning Jesus. This view of the relation of faith and history doe
not allow for a rationalistic construction of the meaning of history
Gregor Smith, as he readily admits, stands closer to Karl Popper a
this point than he does to the more traditional Christian views o
history. He agrees with Popper that history does not present us wit
a discernible pattern of meaning. History has a meaning only as w
give it one. However, unlike Popper, he believes that the meanin
which is given history, so to speak, is not the consequence merely c
our own resolution. Such would be ruled out by Gregor Smith'
critique of secularism. The meaning of history is, rather, given i
the self-understanding of faith, when on the basis of the past th

[15] Dietrich Bonhoeffer, *Ethics* (New York: S.C.M. Press, 1962), p. 61. C
the letter of July 16, 1944, in Bonhoeffer, *Letters and Papers from Prison* (Lor
don: S.C.M. Press, 1953), and the commentary by Gregor Smith in *Worl
Come of Age* (Philadelphia: Fortress, 1967), pp. 18 ff.

believer lives freely for the future. When asking for the meaning of words such as "claims," "forgives," and "grace," we are directed to look into that history of which our history is the concrete manifestation and there, it is said, we will be met by the presence of God, which gives history its meaning. In challenging the world views of secularism, in following the process of secularization through to its limits, Gregor Smith seeks to awaken man to the possibility which is realized in faith's openness to the liberating word in Christ. The meaning of history, then, is given in the recurring moment when a man freely decides his future, and it is this man who is said to be truly autonomous, truly secular.

Discussions of the idea of God are inseparable from discussions of the theory and meaning of the language of religion. A review of the demythologizing controversy and of the discussions by analytical philosophers of the language of religion make this obvious. The basic problem raised can be put in the form of a question: How can language, which is adapted to discourse about things in the world, refer to God without either reducing God to an object alongside other objects in the world or reducing God to a mere projection of the human psyche? Gregor Smith did not live to complete his response to this question. But it is one with which he continually struggled, and there are indications in his last work that he was beginning to see that the problem of the meaning of God is focused in the problem of how we speak about God. Here and elsewhere we can discover the direction in which he was going in order to seek a solution to the question regarding the language of religion.

It is clear that he wishes to divorce himself from mythological and classical theistic attempts to speak of God in such a way that God is objectified and put at the disposal of man. Thus, he agrees with van Buren and the whole tradition of negative theology regarding the necessity of silence about God as he is in himself. We cannot assume a neutral point outside God in order to speak of him in a universally valid way. All such efforts, according to Gregor Smith, make God into an object of knowledge and thus lose his transcendence.

Does this mean then that the word "God" has only a negative meaning? It would if it were not for the possibility of speaking of God's acting, God's encountering man in history. In agreement with

Wilhelm Hermann, Gregor Smith argues that we cannot speak of God in himself but only of what God does to us here and now, and this is disclosed in God's being-for-us in Christ. What God is in himself remains a mystery, and this is essential in order that his transcendence not be lost. Nevertheless, God is not merely the unknown and the mysterious. If we cannot speak of him in his fullness, his being-for-himself, we do have an inkling of his fullness through what he is for us. "Even in our relation with someone whom we know and love there is a surrounding mystery. The other reveals himself to me as one who is there for me out of his incomprehensible fulness. I cannot grasp this fulness, what we may perhaps call his being-for-himself, but I can only have an inkling of it through what he is for me. In an analogous way we cannot grasp the fulness of God's being, we can only have an inkling of it through what he is for us."[16]

It seems, then, that God can be spoken of only in the context of human existence, in the way in which we encounter God's acting toward us. And the language appropriate to this situation, according to Gregor Smith, is the "language of address and response, of man being addressed and his responding."[17] This does not mean, however, that language of God is reduced to the so-called personal model of Martin Buber or John Robinson. The personal model is not wrong so far as it goes, but it does not go far enough. God is not merely an It. But he is also more than a Thou. The whole meaning of the word "God" cannot be unpacked in the person-to-person relationship, for God constitutes and enables the genuine person-to-person relationship. God is the gift, the grace which makes possible man's engagement with man.

The language of God which Gregor Smith is proposing is a historical speaking, a pointing to a dimension within human existence which is more than human existence. We talk in symbols and point to a reality which rises up out of history, which summons us, addresses us. Thus, sentences such as "God is love" are not statements subject to empirical verification. They are, rather, pointers into the revelatory situation, and as such are inseparable from the historical

[16] *Doctrine of God*, p. 160; *Secular Christianity*, pp. 121–123.
[17] *Doctrine of God*, p. 163.

ontext in which they are spoken. Such sentences both point to and make up part of the total revelatory situation in which man encounters the otherness of God within time.[18]

The full implications of this historical speaking of God are not developed by Gregor Smith. But this much can be said: If he avoids the tendency to objectify God by aligning himself with the *via negativa*, he also seeks to avoid the existentialist tendency to reduce language of God to a description of subjective experience. At the same time, he is struggling to avoid the tendency in negative theology to obliterate all connections between historical and perceptual language and the language of God, a tendency which usually results in a failure to say anything of significance about God. According to Gregor Smith, the language of God cannot refer to a worldly phenomenon capable of being observed. But it must refer to a real occurrence, the actual confrontation with an otherness rising up out of history and calling our being into question. In one sense, we are unable to speak about God. We are left in silence in the face of the limits of human possibility. But out of the unfathomable depth which lies beyond this limit "there comes what we do know, and believe, and can talk about, namely, God for us in his historical being in Christ. We cannot know or believe or talk about anything else when we try to speak of God."[19]

The road which Gregor Smith is traveling here is not a simple one. It is filled with pitfalls in every direction. Perhaps no one was more aware of these pitfalls than he. But he struggled persistently, even heroically, to face the difficulties head on. His posthumous book, *The Doctrine of God*, is a testimony to this spirit.

[18] *Secular Christianity*, p. 27; *Doctrine of God*, pp. 164 ff.
[19] *Doctrine of God*, p. 180.

2

Faith and Secularity

SCHUBERT M. OGDEN
Southern Methodist University

Ronald Gregor Smith remains distinguished among his contemporaries for his earnest wrestling with the problem of faith and secularity and for his important contribution toward its solution. In large part, of course, his contribution consists in having mediated to our English-speaking discussion insights relevant to the problem in the thought of such Continental theologians as Rudolf Bultmann, Friedrich Gogarten, and Dietrich Bonhoeffer. But in the more constructive phase of his work, which was cut off so tragically there are clear signs that he was more and more approaching the problem in his own way—a way marked by nothing so much as a willingness to face the problem in all its complexity without the assumptions that oversimplify it and render it insoluble. I do not doubt, therefore, that he would have welcomed my present efforts and, despite their limitations, would have recognized them as yet another indication of the deep community of theological intention between us.

There is a second and closely related reason for my choice of themes. It is my judgment, just as it was Gregor Smith's, that the problem of faith and secularity, assuming "faith" to mean precisely Christian faith in God, is *the* problem of contemporary theology. If one judges from the witness of faith of traditional Christianity then faith's one crucial affirmation is the reality of God as revealed to us in Jesus Christ. Therefore, to be responsible for the Christian witness as the theologian is called to do is to concern oneself above all with this affirmation and with its adequate interpretation in and for the present. Yet just this is impossible today unless one takes account of the claims of a secular understanding of man and the world; for the more seriously one seeks to think and speak in the present and for its sake, the more certainly he discovers his own secularity and that of his time. One must inevitably conclude, then, that our basic theological problem is the exact relation between Christian faith in God and a secular understanding of existence. Since by the nature of the case this problem is bewilderingly complex, it allows for a wide variety of approaches and justifies repeated attempts to solve it. But, most of all, it demands that we make every effort to see that it itself is not so formulated that any real solution to it is already foreclosed.

Which brings us to a third reason for the theme of this essay. Any hope of solving our theological problem depends on recognizing that the terms "faith" and "secularity," rather than certain others with which they are often in effect confused, are the only terms in which the problem is properly formulated. Here I fall back on a fundamental conviction as the only sound approach to theological and philosophical questions. Although we can never approach such questions except as historically conditioned thinkers and thus in the context of our own intellectual tradition and situation, it is nevertheless fatal to assume that any stage of this tradition, past or present, is final. Since all philosophical and theological reflection is exactly that—our effort to *reflect on* our own more basic existential faith or experience—it must always be treated as the secondary thing it in fact is and referred back to the primary reality to which it is always only more or less adequate. All basic thought moves back and forth between our primary faith or experience, which is indubitably real, though only vaguely understood, and our secondary attempts to reflect on it, which add understanding, but only at the price of abstracting from the full concreteness of our experience itself and easily falling into contradiction either with our experience or within and between themselves. So far as our present problem is concerned, this means that we have to avoid two widespread assumptions which so oversimplify the problem that they make it insoluble—at least for anybody unwilling to consider eliminating the poles of the problem as a way of solving it. I refer to the familiar assumptions that one can be truly secular only by accepting some version or other of modern secularism and that one can believe in God only by accepting the claims of what may fairly be called classical theism. Because of these oversimplifying assumptions, the terms of our problem as it is usually discussed are not "faith" and "secularity," but, rather, "classical theism" and "secularism"—and whether or not these particular words are ever used. My contention is that, since the problem is insoluble in these conventional terms, it behooves us to ask whether there are any other terms in which it can be formulated. The theme I have chosen for this essay serves to emphasize and to epitomize my own positive answer to this question.

The purpose of what follows, then, is threefold: (1) to show that there are, in fact, these two assumptions which in effect exclude a solution to our theological problem; (2) to make clear why they are oversimplifications that we have good reason to reject; and (3) to suggest what possibilities open up for solving our problem once we reject them. Since my interest is entirely in an adequate formulation of the problem itself, I have no intention of settling any of the issues I shall raise and will be quite content if I can succeed merely in indicating an approach to the problem that is worth pursuing. Beyond this general caution, two special points should be kept in mind. First, I make no pretense at an exhaustive characterization of any of the phenomena to be considered. For example, the characteristics of secularity as I shall present them are not offered as the only or even the most essential of such defining characteristics. I have reason to think that what I see secularity to be is indeed essential to it and worth taking seriously. But I have no doubt that there is much that would need to be added to my characterization—and that goes for the other things I shall characterize as well. Second, in speaking of "secularism" and of "classical theism," I have no particular philosophical or theological positions in mind. There seem to me to be any number of philosophers or theologians whose basic positions could be fairly described as "secularist" or "classical theist" respectively. Yet, as I use the terms, they are strictly heuristic, in that they designate certain ideal types—certain characteristic belief-systems or integral structures of belief, which can find, and have found, quite diverse forms of expression in the philosophies or theologies of particular men.

Faith as Faith in God

The first step in the argument is to take up an objection to its basic assumption. This is the objection that Christian faith is, first of all, faith in Christ and therefore cannot be properly understood simply as faith in God. Theism in a broad sense is nothing distinctively Christian, and there are other religions and philosophies which have either anticipated Christian belief in God or else given it independent expression. Hence the essential ingredient for Christianity is not simply faith in God, but the unique event of Jesus Christ whereby such faith alone becomes really possible. To reply to this objection fully would require going into the whole issue of the Christocentrism of Christian faith and theology, and would take us well beyond the limits of this essay. But if we are to proceed without excessive risks of misunderstanding, at least this much must be said.

Certainly, in some sense of the word, any faith and theology that are Christian are and must be "Christocentric." So evident is this that there should not be the least question that the sole norm, finally, for determining what is and is not Christian faith in God is the witness of faith of Jesus Christ. Thus, we can readily agree that it is indeed the event of Christ, as the witness of Jesus received by a witnessing community, which is the essential thing for Christianity. The Christ-event is thus essential, namely, insofar as it is precisely through it that the faith in God to which the Christian community bears witness is decisively, even if not exclusively, re-presented as man's authentic possibility. Simply put, what God is for man and what man can be for God is all summed up in Jesus Christ.

Nor is this to say merely that the event of Christ is the decisive historical definition of faith as an original possibility of human existence. To be sure, when it is critically interpreted, the Christian witness so clarifies the meaning of existence that every man, simply as a man, is seen always to have two basic possibilities for self-understanding. On the one hand, he has the possibility of authentic faith in God alone, and thus an existence in radical freedom—both *from* himself and his world, because nothing is ultimately significant save for God's everlasting love for it; and *for* himself and others, because within the boundless scope of God's love everything is of infinite worth. On the other hand, each man has the possibility of that inauthentic faith in God which is idolatry, and which, therefore, is existence in bondage—both to himself and to others, in that he is fully free neither from them nor for them. But beyond thus clarifying or defining man's original possibilities for understanding his existence, the Christian witness claims something else—or, really, two things.

It claims, first, that the existence of man as we actually experience it both in ourselves and in all our fellows discloses that the faith by which we tend to live is not authentic faith in God alone but the inauthentic faith of idolatry. The evidence for this claim, which is traditionally expressed by means of the doctrine of original sin, is that our life is characterized not by genuine freedom but by bondage under all the worldly powers to which we idolatrously attach the ultimate significance of our life—our own health and virtue, the approval of other persons, the success and prosperity of ourselves and our nation, or what have you. Because our faith is thus divided between God and these other powers, we are also divided against ourselves and from one another. We spend our lives in the service of idols, and thus are inconstant in hope, wavering between illusion and despair, and narrow in love, loving only those who love us and serve our gods. And even if it sometimes happens that we are brought to ourselves and enabled once again to lead an authentic life, we experience this precisely as a liberation, as a being set free from the existence in which we normally find ourselves and into which we again and again tend to fall.

Yet the second claim of the Christian witness, which, so far as its importance is concerned, is really first, is that this liberation does in fact take place and is always a real possibility for literally every human being. Although men universally fall into idolatry and so forfeit their possibility of authentic faith, God nevertheless remains God, again and again asserting the sovereignty of his love over all the worldly powers and continually creating that possibility anew. Thus, not even our repeated failure to lay hold of our own humanity can set an insuperable barrier to its attainment. Because the love of God is sovereign over even these failures, embracing even our sin within its scope, our life is freely offered to us anew in every present, and we are once again claimed by the gift and the demand of the First Commandment: "I am the Lord thy God; thou shalt have no other gods besides me." Hence, whoever we are or whatever our situation, we are never without the possibility of authentic faith. We never escape the demand of God's love, nor can we ever be cut off from its gift of new life, which is always given to us if only we are willing to receive it.

And just this is what is decisively re-presented to us through Jesus Christ: not only our original possibility of authentic faith, but also the act whereby God reestablishes this possibility in spite of our idolatry as individuals and as a race. Hence the Christ-event is the definition of faith in God only in that it is also, and more concretely, that faith's one essential sacrament: the sign given in the very midst of human history that God even now embraces all creation within his boundless love and thereby establishes for us and for all mankind the possibility of authentic faith.

But if this is what it means to say that Christian faith is faith in Christ, surely there is no reason to question that it may and must be understood as essentially faith in God. To be sure, the God in whom Christian faith believes is none other than the God and Father of our Lord Jesus Christ, whose gift and demand are decisively defined by the witness of faith of Jesus and his church. Furthermore, Christian faith in this God is not simply theistic belief, if by that is meant intellectual assent to the general truths that there is such a God and that he so acts towards men as to confront them continually with the claim of his love. Christian faith, rather, goes beyond such theism as the concrete exceeds the abstract, insofar as it is existential trust in the love of God *in actu* and *pro me*, of which the event of Christ is the effective sign or sacrament. Yet, for all of its Christocentrism, or, better, just because of it, faith in Christ is clearly nothing other than a certain kind of faith in God—the kind, namely, which trusts and believes and also bears witness that the encompassing mystery of our existence is neither an empty void nor a consuming enmity, but a boundless love, the unconditional acceptance whereby "the creation itself will be set free from its bondage to de-cay and obtain the glorious liberty of the children of God" (Romans 8:21).

Secularity and Secularism

The first of the two assumptions whereby such faith in God is currently rendered problematic is that one can be secular only by also being a secularist. To expose the untenableness of this assumption, I begin by offering a definition of secularity in terms of three essential characteristics.

First, secularity is an understanding of man and the world, of time and history, and of our relations to one another and to nature—an understanding which involves the affirmation of the full reality and significance of these entities. The more popular way of talking about this is to speak simply of the emphatic "this-worldliness" of secular culture. So far as the secular man is concerned, whatever is real or significant must of necessity include his present life in this world. If there be any reality beyond this world, it is not to be invidiously compared with the world as being somehow deficient in reality and inferior in value. What is real either is or includes the temporal and historical reality that makes up our common life; and such values as there are are either identical with or fully inclusive of the values of our life with one another and with the larger life of nature of which we are a part.

Second, secularity involves an insistence on the full autonomy of the various fields of culture (science, art, morality, politics, etc.) over against the field of religion and the claims implied in religious beliefs, actions, and institutions. In this connection, we may recall that the word "secularization" seems to have been originally used to describe the process whereby goods or persons are separated from a previous religious function or control—as, for example, when property is transferred from ecclesiastical to civil ownership or use, or when clergy are changed from regular to secular, or even to lay, status. More broadly, secularization—as the process of becoming secular—involves the establishment of the whole of man's cultural life in its independence from religious or ecclesiastical control, and, concomitantly, the differentiation of religion as itself one field of culture among others. Thus, science, for instance, has come to be pursued solely in terms of its own immanent norms and methods, irrespective of the claims of religious beliefs and the efforts of religious institutions to set limits on its pursuit. Or we may take morality, which is now established as similarly autonomous over against religious definitions of what is obligatory and forbidden. So far as the secular man is concerned, on subjects falling within the sphere of science and open to investigation by its methods, science alone is the arbiter; and what should or should not be done is properly determined solely by reference to the immanent norms and procedures of our moral reason itself. If something is morally good or right, it is so whatever religion may have to say on the matter, and the same holds good for what is scientifically true, aesthetically beautiful, or politically sound.

Finally, secularity involves the methodological conviction that the only ultimate authority for human thought and action in all its forms is man's own shared experience and rational reflection. This is not to say, of course, that the secular man supposes he can live by his own reason and experience alone, apart from the nurture and guidance of his cultural past. The point is simply that, while he recognizes penultimate authorities in the form of the traditions and institutions of human culture, he is convinced that their normativeness is consuetudinary only, not ultimate. They are all open to revision on the basis of the twofold criterion of rational consistency and congruence with human experience critically interpreted. Hence, so far as the secular man is concerned, what proves to be unreasonable or without sufficient basis in experience is thereby reft of any binding claim on his mind and conscience; and this is how he regards it, no matter how venerable it may be and regardless of the formal institutional authority that happens to prop it up.

If I am right, these three characteristics are among the more prominent features of the self-understanding that makes so many of us today secular and therefore accounts for our own personal involvement in one of the poles of the basic theological problem of our time. But I now wish to show that secularity as thus defined is, on point after point, something quite different from the secularism, with which, by a common oversimplification, it is often confused.

Typically, the secularist not only affirms the full reality and significance of this world and our life within it, but goes on to deny that there is anything beyond them. Thus, with respect to the first characteristic, he differs from his secular counterpart solely by reason of a denial or a negation. While sharing the positive secular affirmation of the reality and significance of our life in this world, he denies that our life in any way points beyond itself to another divine life. Significantly, however, the secularist's properly secular affirmation is logically independent of his own secularistic denial. The logic of his statements is such that the truth of his denial in no way follows from the truth of his secular affirmation, nor would the falsity of his denial in any way imply the falsity of his affirmation. The only denial logically implied by secularity is the denial that this world is somehow deficient in reality or inferior in value. But the secularist's denial goes well beyond this, stating as it does that this world is the only reality or value that exists.

Likewise, the secularist not only affirms the autonomy of the various fields of culture vis-à-vis religion, but also denies that there can even be such a thing as religion as itself an autonomous field irreducible to any other. On the usual secularistic interpretations, religion is taken to be at most primitive science or primitive morality or perhaps primitive art, and hence is held to be reducible, finally, to some one or combination of these other cultural fields. But, here again, the secularist simply adds a denial to a secular affirmation, which, so far as the logic of his statements is concerned, does not follow from his affirmation and is insofar gratuitous. His denial could be completely false without in any way affecting the truth of his affirmation, since all the affirmation necessarily denies is that the various fields of human culture are not autonomous or independent spheres in their own right.

And so, too, with respect to the third characteristic. The secularist not only affirms that human experience and reason are the only final criterion of meaning and truth, but he also denies that experience and reason warrant anything other than the empirical generalizations of science or the purely tautological formulations of logic and mathematics. In other words, the secularist adds to the secular affirmation of methodological empiricism the positivistic denial that there is any experience other than sense experience. Again, however, his denial by no means follows logically from the affirmation with which he associates it, and it could well be false while his affirmation itself were true. It is one thing to say that experience and reason are our only final criterion of truth. But it is something else to say that science and logic comprise the only truths that can meet this criterion.

Clearly, then, it is intolerable to assume that only the secularist can be secular. As often as it is made, this assumption confuses two things that are really very different. Secularity in its essence is positive, consisting of affirmations of the full reality and significance of our life in this world, of the autonomy of the other fields of culture in relation to religion, and of the final authority of reason and shared experience. Secularism, by contrast, consists in the same affirmations combined with utterly negative denials that by no means follow from them and could very well be false even though the affirmations themselves were true. These are the denials that anything beyond our life in this world is real or significant, that there can be any such thing as religion as itself a cultural field, and that there can be any final source of truth about existence other than empirical science. Since these denials are in no way logically required by secular affirmations, the assumption that secularity can express itself only as secularism should be rejected as the most serious oversimplification of our problem. For, if secularism is true, there can be no solution to the problem of faith and secularity except by simply denying one pole of the problem—namely, faith in the reality of God. On the other hand, if secularism should prove false, this would in no way imply the falsity of secularity, and we might be left with both poles of the problem still intact. So long as secularism is not known to be true, faith in God is still an open question; and secularity is an open question even if secularism is known to be false.

Classical Theism and Faith in God

And so we come to the second of the conventional assumptions which so oversimplify our problem as to preclude its possible solution, namely, that one can have faith in God only by assenting to the truth of the belief-system of classical theism. I hold that what may be distinguished respectively as "classical theism" and "faith in God" are logically related in somewhat the same way as "secularism" and "secularity." Thus, I would like to show, by way of a summary characterization of classical theism, that it is defined not only by the positive affirmation of the reality of God and some related affirmations pertaining to the autonomy of religion and the scope of human experience and reason, but also by certain negative denials that are by no means necessarily implied by the affirmations themselves. To the extent that this can be shown, the problem of faith and secularity will once again turn out to be a more complex problem than it is commonly assumed to be.

The first characteristic of classical theism is that it not only affirms the reality of God as distinct from and more than the reality of the world, whether as individuals or as a collection, but also denies that the world itself is fully real and significant. The basis of this denial is the time-honored premise of the Western theistic tradition that God, as in all respects the perfect or unsurpassable individual, must also be strictly immutable or unchanging and wholly absolute or incapable of relation to others. Were God in any way able to change by being really related to the changing world and so affectible by it, he would not, so the premise holds, really be God. But it follows from this that the world as such is ultimately insignificant and not fully real. With the world or without it, God is still the absolute actualization of all possible reality and value, so that whatever happens in the world, for good or for ill, is, in the final analysis, of no consequence. God can be neither increased nor diminished by the decisions of his creatures, and their action, like their suffering, must be in the strictest sense indifferent to him. Of course, this implication is rarely stated or accepted in the sharp form in which I have expressed it—for the very good reason that it makes utter nonsense of most of what is clearly asserted about God in the Holy Scripture that theologians are supposed to interpret. But a careful reading even of contemporary spokesmen for traditional theism will always turn up an abundance of statements like these:

> The relation between God and his creatures is a wholly one-sided rela-
> tion, in that while the creation depends absolutely upon God, God in no
> sense depends upon his creation. God would be neither more nor less
> perfect if the creation dissolved into utter nothingness. The absolute per-
> fection of perfect being would still exist.
> God added nothing to himself by the creation of the world, nor would
> anything be taken away from him by its annihilation—events which
> would be of capital importance for the created things concerned, but
> null for Being who would be in no wise concerned *qua* being.
> In view of the widespread tendency even among theologians to-day
> to be satisfied with a doctrine of God as in one way or another condi-
> tioned by or dependent on his creation, it is important to stress the ab-
> solute necessity of the conception of the entire independence of God. . . .
> Unless we are prepared to accept the God of classical theism, we may as
> well be content to do without a God at all.[1]

Such statements speak for themselves, though I remark in passing that the concluding sentence is a beautiful example of the oversimplification to which I am here calling attention.

Classical theism involves, second, not only the affirmation that religion is an autonomous field of culture that cannot be reduced to any other, but also the denial that the other cultural fields are in turn fully autonomous. No doubt the easiest way to recognize this denial is simply to recall the central place of the miraculous in the usual expressions of classical theism. Even though modern classical theists may no longer make as many claims as their predecessors, they still insist on a minimal belief in miracle as essential to faith in God, and so are forced to deny the autonomy of science and critical history insofar as they have a bearing on such belief. Thus, Karl

[1] E. L. Mascall, *He Who Is: A Study in Traditional Theism* (London: Longmans, Green and Co., 1943), pp. 95 ff. Only the last statement is Mascall's, the others being cited by him from well-known books by Richard Hanson and Etienne Gilson. I owe this reference to Peter Hamilton, *The Living God and the Modern World* (London: Hodder and Stoughton, 1967), p. 31.

Jaspers has rightly complained of theologians who seem quite willing to demythologize the traditional accounts of creation and yet call for an uncritical acceptance of Jesus' physical resurrection as necessary to Christian faith.[2] But belief in the miraculous is certainly not the only evidence of classical theism's denial of cultural autonomy. There is the whole so-called "warfare of science with theology," during which theology has tried to retain a foothold in each of the fields successively claimed by science, only to be forced again and again to beat a retreat. And from the recent past, it is sufficient to remember Pope Paul VI's *Humanae Vitae* to see how ecclesiastical measures can also subvert the autonomy of moral judgment and decision.

Finally, classical theism involves not only the affirmation of a truth beyond the truth of empirical science, but also the denial that human experience and reason are the last instance for deciding what is true in all cases where there is a conflict of claims. This denial, which, like the others mentioned, is essential to traditional theism, rests ultimately on the claim that there are certain religious truths, usually designated *mysteria stricte dicta,* that are in principle beyond the competence of human experience and reason. As truths strictly of revelation and faith, they are in no way amenable to rational assessment, but are to be believed entirely on the authority of the teaching church, or of the Word of God in Scripture as authenticated by the *testimonium internum spiritus sancti.* With this understanding of experience and reason as having, at most, a strictly limited jurisdiction, classical theists may quite naturally be disinclined to submit to them even in matters where they are acknowledged to be competent. In any case, it is not uncommon to find such theists dignifying as a "mystery" to be reverently accepted what most of us would unhesitatingly consider simply a confusion or a contradiction.

So defined, in terms of these three characteristics, classical theism is directly contradictory not only of the negations of the secularist but of the positions of secularity as well. Consequently, if this kind of theism is true, neither secularism nor secularity, for all of their fundamental difference, can also be true. The reason for this is that

    [2] Karl Jaspers and Heinz Zahrnt, *Philosophie und Offenbarungsglaube, Ein Zwiegespräch* (Hamburg: Furche Verlag, 1963), pp. 38 ff.

the affirmations of the classical theist contradict and are contradicted by the denials of the secularist, while the theist's own denials contradict and are contradicted by the affirmations made on behalf of the secular. Recognizing this, we should have no trouble understanding that the affirmation of classical theism, or the assumption that it is the only belief-system in terms of which Christian faith in God can be expressed, has the same kind of effect on our problem as the corresponding assumption in the case of secularism. It has the effect, namely, of excluding any solution to our problem by totally eliminating one of its poles—in this case, the pole of secularity. But perhaps it will be agreed, then, that we have more than sufficient reason to inquire whether here, too, there may not be an unwarranted assumption that drastically oversimplifies the real problem.

That this is in fact the case may seem clear enough simply from the consideration that none of the three denials essential to classical theism follow from the positive affirmation with which it is usually associated. Thus, in order to affirm the reality of God as something more than or distinct from the world, whether as individuals or as a collection, one need not deny that this world itself is fully real and significant. To assume otherwise would be rather like inferring that I can affirm a nonbehavioristic account of my self as something more than the activities of my bodily cells only by denying that these cells themselves are fully real. I am more than my body and distinct from it just because, or insofar as, I include its multiplicity of cellular activities in a new center of activity of a higher order. Of course, the implication of this line of reasoning is that God is to be conceived of as related to the world, or to the multiplicity of beings other than himself, in somewhat the way that we are each related to our own bodies—from which it follows that, by analogy, the world is the body of God even as God is the self of the world. But, aside from the fact that this analogy can be defended as the best clue we have to an adequate theistic position, were one to take such a position he could very well affirm the reality of God while not denying but also affirming the full reality and significance of the world. If whatever is other than God is nevertheless part of God's body, integral to his own divine and everlasting life, then it could not possibly be more real or significant. Nor is the price of taking this position the pantheistic denial that God is essentially other than the world and independent of it. It is merely faulty logic to maintain that God can be an individual in his own right, distinct from all others, only by utterly excluding them. No less individuating is the uniquely divine attribute of all-inclusiveness, which, since it itself includes nothing but is, rather, included in everything, renders God a distinct individual whose existence is totally independent of that of any other. In short, classical theism could be quite false in its denial that the world is fully real and significant, even though a nonpantheistic affirmation of God's reality might very well be true.

Likewise, one need not deny the autonomy of other cultural fields in order to affirm the autonomy of religion. As a matter of fact, to suppose that there is need for such a denial can only imply that religion is open to the very reduction that its secularistic interpreters seek to effect. If religion can be itself only by encroaching on the other fields of culture, then it can evidently be reduced to those fields to the precise extent of such encroachment. Hence, if religion is to be held irreducible, and in that sense autonomous, it must be distinguished as a matter of principle from all of the other cultural fields, which must then be acknowledged to be equally autonomous vis-à-vis religion. To distinguish religion in this manner, however, in no way requires one to violate its own self-understanding as being vastly more important than simply one field of culture alongside several others. It is a sheer *non sequitur* to infer from the fact that things are distinct in principle that they are also coordinate in importance. A whole is evidently distinct from any of its parts, but this hardly implies that it itself is simply one such part. The basic importance of religion, then, far from being a reason why the autonomy of cultural fields should be denied, is the very reason it has to be affirmed.

Finally, affirmation of a truth about existence beyond the truth of science in no way requires the denial that the ultimate criterion of truth is human experience and reason. The contrary supposition is plausible only if the scope of this criterion is assumed to be a good deal more restrictive than it actually is. Provided one recognizes that reflection on our immediate awareness allows for a kind of truth-claim that is distinctively metaphysical, one can insist that experience and reason alone are the ultimate arbiters of truth without implying that scientific truth is the only kind there is. Nor does such insistence commit one to a rationalism for which nothing is strictly mysterious because nothing outreaches reason's grasp. It is simply fallacious to assume that reason and mystery are so related that the more there is of the one the less there must be of the other. In fact, one may argue that the opposite is closer to the truth—that the more rational the metaphysics, the more likely it is to acknowledge its impenetrable limit in the mysterious givenness of our actual existence.

There are good reasons to conclude, then, that the affirmations of classical theism are independent of its characteristic denials, and so cannot be simply identified with them. Even if its negations were all false, the positions of theism could well be true, and we would still have the possibility of a genuine solution to our problem. For, as should now be apparent, all that is positive in theism is contradictory only of the negations of secularism, not of the positions of secularity. Unless classical theism is known to be true, secularity is still an open question, and faith in God is an open question even if classical theism is known to be false.

Faith in God and Secularity

If the argument to this point has achieved its purpose, there should no longer be any question that our problem is a good deal more complex than is generally allowed. Evidently, it will not do to assume either that we can be truly secular only by subscribing to some form of the belief-system of secularism, or that we can believe in God only by accepting the structure of beliefs that constitutes classical theism. And yet, once these common assumptions are exposed for what they are—baseless oversimplifications whereby secularists and classical theists divide the ground between them and survive on one another's weaknesses—the problem of faith and secularity becomes an utterly new and different problem. We are at last free to ask whether it is not possible, after all, to be fully secular and yet affirm all that is really positive in traditional Christian theism.

Obviously, my own inclination is to answer this question affirmatively, and I feel supported in this by a number of other thinkers who have already made important contributions towards defending this answer. But since I can hardly present a defense of it here, I must be content in closing with simply suggesting why it seems to me correct.

Surely there can be little question that the understanding of life here defined as secularity, as distinct from secularism, is itself the fruit of traditional Christian faith and witness. This is not to say, naturally, that modern secularity has no other origin than the witness of Scripture. Many of the recent attempts to show that the Bible—especially the Old Testament—is itself the charter of our modern secular outlook are evidently strained and unconvincing apologetics. Still, there is no reason to doubt that secularity has its roots deep in the synthesis of scriptural religion with the culture of classical antiquity, which was first effected by the Christian apologists of the second century and then attained classical expression in the work of Augustine. By this synthesis, Greek humanism, with its stress on man's reason and autonomy, grew together with the scriptural understanding of the full reality and significance of time and history until, with the Renaissance and the Reformation, the fruit of modern secularity began to ripen. All of which I take to indicate that a secular understanding of life, far from being antithetical to faith in God, may well be its most appropriate expression. To affirm that life here and now is fully real and significant, that the various fields of culture are to be respected in their autonomy, and that human experience and reason are our only final court of appeal —in short, to affirm all that secularity positively affirms, seems to me just what one would affirm if he had a correspondingly positive faith in the God revealed in Jesus Christ. For this God is the One for whom whatever is is of imperishable significance, whose sole claim on his creatures is that they become fully themselves, and who, being universally present in everything that is so much as even possible, cannot but be attested by all that we can experience or think.

But scarcely less certain, at least to me, is that secularity tends by its own inner dynamism towards explicit faith in God. To affirm the significance and autonomy of this world and to insist on the rights and responsibility of human experience and reason is to speak out of an underlying confidence in the worth of life that theistic belief alone can make fully explicit. This assumes, of course, that one can and indeed must distinguish between theism as such and the classical theism of our philosophical-theological tradition, with its gratuitous negations. But if by "theism" one means the positive affirmations of the reality of God, of the irreducibility of religion, and of a truth about existence beyond the truth of science, it seems to me the only way to a secularity that is fully self-conscious, in that it grasps reflectively and explicitly the basic faith in the worth of life that it itself implies.

3

Tradition as a Theological Concept

WILLIAM MCKANE
University of St. Andrews

Given the opportunity of contributing to this volume in memory of Ronald Gregor Smith, I cannot altogether disengage myself from the peculiarly deep personal relationship which I had with him nor can I stifle the instinct to indulge in biographical reminiscence. I saw him and had conversation with him nearly every day during the last years at Glasgow. Although our fields of scholarship were different and we were, in some respects, far apart temperamentally, I encountered in him a humanity rich and yet austere, more tragic and more authentic than I have known in any other person.

I greatly admired his elegance of expression and the mysterious beauty of his style of writing, and, while my level of achievement fell short of his, this was a field of creative literary endeavor which I understood and shared with him. We were united by a common fascination and reverence for words. We did not often discuss theology, certainly not in a way that would have debased our conversation and made our meetings into mini-seminars. Although Gregor Smith had a relish for theological discussion and was at his best in the right kind of group, he disliked the formalizing of discussion into debate and would never agree to appear as a protagonist for Christianity. As he often said, he had no stomach for defending "positions," and knockabout debates between Christians and humanists he regarded as barren. This, too, explains why he was distressed and puzzled by what seemed to him merely destructive criticisms of his own work. He was much too sensitive for his own comfort and could not hide the marks of his wounds, but, when he was relaxed, his

44

attitudes in theological discussion were essentially positive. However much he might disagree with a paper, he never had any inclination to kill discussion prematurely by some devastating negative criticism. He conceived his role, rather, as that of seizing upon such positive aspects as he could discover and advancing the discussion by developing those aspects.

However diverse might be the verbal expressions of our respective theologies, I have no doubt that the basis of our relationship was a deep affinity of theological style. Gregor Smith's ultimate theological seriousness was incompatible with a conventional seriousness of discourse, and he found relief from the awful clarity of his vision in a humor which had the delectable dryness of his wine and an irony, gentle and not so gentle, occasionally savage and touched with the macabre. Younger than he and his junior colleague, I was greatly stirred by the circumstance that he trusted me so absolutely and shared his confidences with me. I owed much in those days to his generosity of spirit and, I might almost say, to his patronage, for I shall always regard myself as having been in a strange and indirect way his protégé. It is only in the wake of his death and as a consequence of the distance which now separates me from the living relationship which I had with him that I am able to understand the richness of that friendship. It is therefore *con amore* and with treasured memories of the hospitality which I enjoyed in his home and the quiet conversation which I had with him and his wife that I address myself to this task.

Since the exploration of tradition as a theological concept in the Old Testament has been one of my interests, it is natural that I should turn to the long section on tradition in Gregor Smith's last book.[1] It was on this theological ground that my own interests and his tended to meet, and with his accustomed kindness to me he has revealed some evidences of the small influence which I may have had on his thinking, although it would be a mistake to suppose that there is anything uncharacteristic in his discerning probing of the implications of tradition or that it is in any way incompatible with the radical strain in his theology.

[1] Ronald Gregor Smith, *The Doctrine of God* (London: Collins, 1970).

It was, I think, my abiding interest in Gerhard von Rad's *Theo-logie*[2] that directed his attention towards the sage of Heidelberg, and he rightly saw in his work insights comparable to those which Rudolf Bultmann, whom he knew so well and so greatly admired, had applied to the New Testament. That Gregor Smith should attach such importance to a theological evaluation of tradition will surprise only those who suppose that his radicalism was a brash, superficial form of innovation, innocent and unperceptive of the historical depth of Christianity. It will surprise those who are not aware that he was fundamentally a biblical and apostolic theologian and who confuse theological courage with instant reinterpretations of Christianity. Like Bultmann, he held that there could be no authentic existence without a long historical memory, and his roots were deep in the rich soil of Western civilization. He was an eminently civilized theologian, a complete European, and it is not insignificant that he was particularly at home in the eighteenth century, the age of reason. He was not susceptible to the Romantic fallacy, for he, and especially his wife, had seen too much of Nazism not to know the dangers of Romanticism.

He had journeyed far beyond any theology based on a dichotomy of revelation and reason, and there was in him a hardness of logic characteristic of the lowland Scot and a skepticism which linked him to David Hume, that ornament of eighteenth-century Edinburgh whose brilliant intellectual life so fascinated Gregor Smith. This element of cool reason may serve to explain how it was that one of unusual aesthetic sensitivity combined the originality of his vision and the poetry of his theology with a lack of sympathy for mysticism which he thought inimical with the essential stance of Christian faith. All of this entered into the texture of his secularity, which was concerned with man in his modernity, inseparable in his mind from man in relation to his past. He did not believe in "revolutions" in theology, because he knew that continuity is as central a theological problem as modernity and that superficial, *de novo* reconstructions

[2] Gerhard von Rad, *Theologie des Alten Testaments.* Bd. I, *Die Theologie der geschichtlichen Überlieferungen Israels* (München: Chr. Kaiser Verlag, 1957). Bd. II, *Die Theologie der prophetischen Überlieferungen Israels* (München: Chr. Kaiser Verlag, 1960). D. M. G. Stalker, trans., *Old Testament Theology* (Edinburgh: Oliver and Boyd), vol. 1 (1962), vol. 2 (1965).

do not deal seriously with the historical and contingent elements in Christianity. For him, keeping the faith was the same as remaining truly human, and Christianity was an authentic humanism. A modern theology is necessarily one which deals with the past and the problem of transmission, and from this germ of concern there grew his subtle and complex evaluation of tradition.

It is entirely fitting that his last book contains the substance of lectures which he was to have given at Princeton Theological Seminary, for his abiding concern was for the "reformation" of the Gospel. The semester which he had spent at McCormick Theological Seminary was an experience about which he frequently talked. The American scene greatly stirred and animated him, and he was encouraged by the spirit of the open and adventurous theological inquiry in which he was caught up. Although he seriously considered an academic appointment in America, it always seemed to me that he was right to hold himself back from it. He had the warmest regard for America, and his visits there were a necessary catharsis, a release from the conventional primness and theological timidity which he found in some places at home and which he could not endure, but his spiritual home was Europe.

Tradition for Gregor Smith was not a stuffy, conservative concept nor an embodiment of norms and guarantees, but rather the form of a theological problem. His definition of the problem is admirably illustrated by his allusion to the debate between Lessing and Pastor Goeze.[3] He knew that Christian theology cannot escape from the particular and contingent, and therefore from what might appear to be a hopeless imprisonment, into the philosophical security of timeless and universal truths. If the Gospel cannot then be disengaged from its pastness, from its temporal and local limitations, how can it be understood and expressed as the truth in relation to our human situation after the passage of two millennia?

Gregor Smith's mind was not one that was specially drawn to the particularities and niceties of biblical-critical scholarship, yet he took the Bible seriously, and one of the reasons why Bultmann had a unique place in his regard and affection was that Gregor Smith discerned in Bultmann a mastery of the *Kleinigkeiten* of New Testa-

[3] *The Doctrine of God*, p. 41 ff.

ment scholarship combined with the rare ability of raising these *Kleinigkeiten* to a level of theological significance. He therefore understood the theological significance of *Überlieferungsgeschichte* in Bultmann, and the various expressions of his hermeneutical interest, from demythologizing, through the subtle and difficult discussion of "history" in *Secular Christianity*,[4] to his positive attitude towards tradition in *The Doctrine of God*, derive from his recognition that there is nothing more ultimate for Christianity than the New Testament witness and that it is not possible to get behind this witness in order to achieve a *de novo* reconstruction of "the events themselves."

In this sense he was a theologian of the Word, only it must not be thought that he was a biblical or kerygmatic theologian in any restrictive sense or that any antithesis between reason and revelation is implied in his being a theologian of the Word. Like Bultmann, he was absorbed in the peculiar problems involved in "knowing" ancient documents in the context of our distance in time from these documents. This he expressed in terms of a dialectic between their pastness and our presentness, between a knowledge of the Word and knowledge of ourselves. Hence there is nothing authoritative or normative in his concept of tradition, for the rescue of the Word from unintelligibility or incredibility may demand the boldest of reinterpretations. But more important than the exercise of judgment on matters of detail are the essentials of his concept of tradition. Tradition is not an anodyne for timid or nervous Christians or a justification of ecclesiastical absolutism, and there are no final, static, propositional formulations to which one can "subscribe" and thereby "make a confession of faith." On the contrary, faith is the recognition that there is no such finality and that there is no end to the ongoing dialectic between the Word and our self-understanding. In this, no distinction is drawn between Scripture on the one hand and creeds or "subordinate standards" on the other, and so Scripture is not exempted from this dialectic as the "supreme rule of faith," and cannot be used as a source of norms.

[4] Ronald Gregor Smith, *Secular Christianity* (London: Collins, 1966).

Tradition in Old Testament Theology

In the second and major part of this article I turn to certain aspects of Old Testament theology and, in particular, to the theology of the patriarchal stories, in order to further the study of tradition as a theological concept. Although my approach is altogether different, I hope it will be evident that the issues raised by Gregor Smith in his discussion of tradition are at the center of the Old Testament debate. It was the intention of the Göttingen school of *Religionsgeschichte*, of which Hermann Gunkel was a member, that the supernatural should become redundant in theological discussion and that the distinctiveness of biblical religion should be demonstrated without invoking a dichotomy of natural and supernatural.[5] This was an objective which would have commended itself to all scholars who appreciated the full implications of the advent of the critical era for biblical theology, but it was an aspect of the program of *Religionsgeschichte* which raised the hackles of dogmatic theologians who were still unreconciled to the consequences of critical scholarship for the old forms of biblical theology and still persisted in their efforts to distill a propositional theology from the Bible. For the purpose of dogmatics, the Bible was still a book which had fallen out of heaven, a reservoir of revealed truth without historical inlets or outlets, in a word, a supernatural book. Critical scholars like Wellhausen in Germany, S. R. Driver in England, and Robertson Smith in Scotland, to mention only representative figures, knew that this style of Old Testament theology was dead and buried. The Bible had not fallen from heaven like manna; it was a human product, and it had to be studied as a historical document which was exposed to the accidents and contingencies of history.

But the passing of the old propositional, biblical theology has created a problem to which critical scholarship has found no easy answer. Ever since, there has been the greatest uncertainty among

---

[5] See especially Werner Klatt, *Hermann Gunkel: Zu seiner Theologie der Religionsgeschichte und Enstehung der Formgeschichtlichen Methode* (Göttingen: Vandenhoeck and Ruprecht, 1969), pp. 17 ff.

critical scholars as to whether it is proper to speak of an Old Testa
ment theology, and even those who believe this to be meaningfu
have not reached any consensus as to what constitutes an Old Testa
ment theology. In the earlier years of the critical era there woulc
seem to have been no great concern over the demise of Old Testa
ment theology and no sense of urgency about the need to recon
struct a new one. There was so much to do, so many exciting appli
cations of criticism to the problems of biblical scholarship whicl
could be made. The critical method might not be able to deal witl
the matter of a new Old Testament theology, but there was mucl
that could be accomplished, and those tasks which could be accom
modated to the new approach were the ones which seemed academ
ically most respectable and most in need of being done.

The consequences of criticism for Old Testament theology were
in a word, that the raw materials of study became religious idea
rather than doctrines, and these, moreover, were inevitably caugh
up in the flow of historical criticism and could not therefore be
immune from historical relativity. A normative theology cannot be
constructed out of a flow of religious ideas. It would not be unfai
to say that Old Testament scholarship in general has not yet come
to terms with the inevitable theological consequences of the recog
nition that the Old Testament is a book that must be studied criti
cally. That is to say, scholars who are masters of critical methoc
nevertheless persist in the belief that religious ideas which are par
of the historical flow can somehow, for the purpose of exhibiting
them as ideas which are theologically or ethically normative and
perennially valid, be released from the prison of contingency and
acquire a universal and timeless validity. Any theology of the Old
Testament whose content is religious ideas which are presented as
permanently normative is guilty of a final failure of stringency and
a suspension of criticism in the interests of edification. An Old
Testament theology which owes its existence to an act of piety is
really a confession of failure. It is an admission that since the advent
of the critical era Old Testament theology has become impossible.

Whether we take the view of the first edition of Gunkel's *Genesis*
that the patriarchal stories originate in myths, or that of the third
edition, that they originate in *Märchen*, the striking feature of

Gunkel's account from the point of view of *Religionsgeschichte* is that the literary history and the religious history of the stories fall entirely apart from each other.[6] It may be thought that this does not matter and certainly should not be regarded as a damning circumstance, but a closer consideration produces a less sanguine view of the matter. The literary merits of the stories and their narrative vitality are entirely severed from their religious content, so that the form of the stories on which Gunkel lavishes his careful and discerning aesthetic analysis are, according to Gunkel himself, destitute of religious value. Their value as absorbing stories, as imaginative products, as fragrant poetry, bears no relationship to their religious value. This is a great loss.

If religious significance were to be attached to the stories, one would hope that the religion would be in the stories themselves and would be integrated with their total aesthetic effect; that the imaginative forms would themselves be the bearers of religious insights. Instead, the religious content of the stories is said to originate in complete separation from the processes of creative literary composition; they are an accretion of piety, a veneer of edification. It is the "collectors" of the stories, not their creators or even their tellers who confer on them the level of religious refinement of which Gunkel approves. Those who composed the stories and for whose aesthetic achievement Gunkel has the highest praise are nevertheless religious primitives.

It may be questioned whether theology which originates with collectors of stories and which is superimposed in the interests of piety and edification deserves serious consideration. Gunkel's method of *Religionsgeschichte* is in danger here of descending to a level of mere conventional piety. If there is theological vitality in the patriarchal stories, it must be shown to belong to the creative process itself and to be conveyed through the "story." It cannot merely be the addendum of a pious glossarist. What is offered here by Gunkel is subsequent refining or spiritualizing of the stories, and there is the assumption that the theological value of the stories is a consequence of this process. This is the weakness of *Religionsgeschichte*, for it

[6] Hermann Gunkel, *Genesis* (Göttingen: Vandenhoeck and Ruprecht, 1956).

cannot overcome the barrier to Old Testament theology created b
its own critical method. On the one hand, it is a mistaken enterpris
to separate the theological investigation from the total literary ap
preciation of the stories. Let us have the roughness, the earthiness
the secularity of the stories themselves and concentrate the theolog
ical inquiry in this area. The view that the theology has been contrib
uted to the stories not by the creators and tellers of them but by th
later collectors reduces the theology of the stories to a precious piety
and the value which is attached to the process depends on a theoret
ical concept of spirituality, an assumption about what constitute
superior religious ideas which is not to be accepted.

On the other hand, there is the more fundamental philosophica
problem. If the religious value of the stories is described in this way
they are doomed to theological oblivion. If Old Testament theolog
is concerned with a progression or flow of religious ideas, an ascen
from lower to higher, then everything has been swallowed up by th
passage of time; the whole has been made obsolete. Religious idea
which were superior in the age of the collectors of the patriarcha
stories would inevitably with the passage of time become inferio
and so on *ad infinitum*. One might wish to posit certain historica
points of high attainment, to say that at these times peaks of spir
itual and moral achievement were reached and to prize these ideas a
normative forever. But there is no such escape from the method o
Religionsgeschichte. If what constitutes Old Testament theology i
a system of superior religious ideas, these ideas are part of the his
torical flow and cannot be abstracted from it. In saying that th
higher religious ideas were superadded to the patriarchal stories b
collectors one is already indicating the transience of these ideas an
condemning them to obsolescence.

It is out of considerations such as these that tradition becomes ar
important concept for Old Testament theology (and, of course, fo
New Testament theology as well). Tradition is a central concern
because transmission is a problem. This is not a matter about th
technical aspects of transmission; it is not merely about how th
stories have been preserved so that we can read them today. It is
rather, a question about how they can address us today in a mean
ingful way. It is a consideration of how they have been able to

retain their theological seriousness and vitality down through the generations. We may not be able to answer these questions, and certainly we cannot answer them at this stage of the inquiry. There are, however, certain negative conclusions which have been reached. The patriarchal stories cannot possess theological seriousness for me if the content of their theology is defined as higher religious ideas which were worked into the stories by those who collected them. The theological problem of tradition is such that there can be no dichotomy of *Literaturgeschichte* and *Religionsgeschichte*. The theological seriousness of the story for me, if it has any, is not separable from the total impact of the story, that is, the narrative power, the fitness of characterization, and the aesthetic effects.

The demand for a unitary account embracing both *Literaturgeschichte* and *Religionsgeschichte* or, rather, *Theologie* is satisfied by Martin Noth. In respect to theology, the most important adjustment is the shift of emphasis from religious ideas to credal affirmation, but this does not signify the reinstatement of a dogmatic Old Testament theology. The seed of the patriarchal stories is a credal article ("A wandering Aramaean was my father," Deuteronomy XXVI: 5) which is a reference to Jacob; the theology and the narrative are inseparable at the point of origin, and the tradition of the stories is throughout a unitary process without any dichotomy of literary and theological components. It is true that, according to Noth, there is a slackening of the connection of the stories from their original credal and cultic concerns, but the account of their tradition still remains, nevertheless, a single one. What may be questioned here in Noth is his view that the stories become less theological because they are detached from sanctuaries and from credal claims of which they are vehicles earlier in the history of the tradition.

Thus, according to Noth, the west Jordan Jacob traditions give expression to the claims of the Israelite tribes to possess the land of Canaan. The Promise made to the cult founder Jacob by his god has been fulfilled for the Israelite tribes by Yahweh, and the patriarchal stories have in this way been integrated with another article of Israel's creed, the assertion that Yahweh gave the Israelites the land of Canaan. Thus the settlement tradition appears as the ful-

fillment of the patriarchal traditions. These west Jordan Jacob tra
ditions further Israel's claim to Canaan by representing that the
patriarch had connections with Canaanite sanctuaries which, after
the settlement, were centers of assembly and of credal affirmation
for Israelite tribes.

The east Jordan stories are no longer dominated by these claims
nor are they stories about the associations of the patriarch with an
cient Canaanite sanctuaries. They are more mundane and earthy
and reflect the more general concerns of coexistence between the
Ephraimite colonists in east Jordan and their Aramaean neighbors
The title to the land of Canaan is no longer an issue. The frictions
which arise in the process of cultural change within the one community are, on the other hand, reflected in the stories about Jacob
and Esau.

This is an illuminating account in respect to *Literaturgeschichte*,
and it shows that the stories are undergoing a literary transformation
in their passage from west Jordan to east Jordan. What should be
asked, however, is whether this liberation from sanctuaries and
credal concerns is an indication of a loss of theological content or
whether it is not, rather, evidence of the acquisition of a new kind of
theological content. The secularity of the stories, the absence of
sanctuaries and theophanies, the dominance of pressing everyday
concerns, the new liberty given to the characters in these stories to
assert their freedom, to make mistakes, to be overcome by evil, to
explore the labyrinthine recesses of their humanity—all of this
should be understood and assessed not as the disappearance of
theology but as evidence of a new theology.

The development of this insight constitutes part of von Rad's
originality as an Old Testament theologian. According to von Rad,
the patriarchal stories in so far as they are local and cultic and have
their point and power in their attachment to sanctuaries had become irrelevant and impotent at the period when the Yahwist gave
a new structure to the complex of traditions with which he worked.[7]

[7] See especially Gerhard von Rad, *Das Erste Buch Mose, Genesis* (Göttingen:
Vandenhoeck and Ruprecht, 1956). John H. Marks, trans., *Genesis: A Com
mentary* (London: S.C.M. Press, 1961), pp. 27 ff.

their effective functioning at the centers to which they had belonged had presupposed an immediacy of cultic participation, a
more naïve age when theophanies were the raw material of theology.
In so far as the stories are merely locally bound tales about sanctuaries which have acquired holiness and terror as a consequence of
appearances of Yahweh to the patriarchs at these sanctuaries, they
have no longer a high theological seriousness in the reign of Solomon. The Yahwist addressed his theology to the intellectual climate of that age and so related the patriarchal stories to the whole of
his theology of the Hexateuch that he released the sanctuary stories
from their local limitations and from the divinized world to which
they originally belonged and gave them a new level of significance in
theology which is marked by its secularity and its fitness for the
"humanism" of the Solomonic enlightenment.

Yahweh is no longer the God of the theophany whose effective
working is to be correlated with his appearances at special times and
places, yet Yahweh has fulfilled his Promise to Israel, almost, it
might seem, by doing good by stealth, remaining hidden and yet
making Israel into an empire with its tenure of Canaan uncontested
and with a secure place in the world. There is a secularity about this
fulfillment. It can be explained in terms of David's military ability
and political acumen; it seems only too worldly, the product of
human cleverness and ambition; and the style of life which it ushers
in is a confident humanism. Its cultural products are historiography
which stems from a sense of national pride and achievement and a
composition like the Joseph story (Genesis XXXVII: 1) which reveals an openness to the themes of a literature of international wisdom.[8] The Joseph story and the Rebekah story (Genesis XXIV) are
particularly revealing examples of the civilization and theological
temper of the age of the Yahwist. It is a time which makes room for
the full expression of human capacities and activities, a time in
which men act decisively and effectively in order to shape their

---

[8] Gerhard von Rad, "Josephgeschichte und altere Chokma," *Supplement to
Vetus Testamentum*, I (1953), pp. 120–127. E.W.T. Dicken, trans., *The
Problem of the Hexateuch and Other Essays* (Edinburgh: Oliver and Boyd,
1966), pp. 292–300.

world. No longer do they await or expect the intervention of God at every critical juncture. Because they have this freedom and power there is a vast new area of human interest accessible to literature.

Theology need no longer be dominated by Yahweh, and yet this is not the demise of theology, for this fulfillment in all its secularity is that which is affirmed in the old creed (Deuteronomy XXVI: 5–9) and the Promise which has been fulfilled is none other than that which is heard in the patriarchal stories. After disappointments, dangers, and mediocrity the dominant possession of Canaan has at last been achieved and this, von Rad suggests, was a theological discovery. The settlement tradition, the final resounding article of the creed (Deut. XXVI: 9), had begun to sound hollow against the difficulties of Israel's early days in Canaan. Disorganization, disunity, and weakness in the face of danger did not correspond with the affirmation that Yahweh had given Israel the land of Canaan. The old creed, which no longer had its cultic anchorage or the social and theological climate which supported its life, seemed no more than a matter of antiquarian interest, but it was then brought to life and restored to vigor in the new context of the Davidic fulfillment.

There are two general observations which can be made about this treatment of the theology of the Hexateuch. In the first place, there is the discovery of the significance of context. A widening of context can bring about a change in theological meaning. This has repercussions for Old Testament theology beyond the limits of the Hexateuch, as is evident from von Rad's treatment of the theme of Promise. The possibilities of Promise can be stretched out beyond the Davidic fulfillment and may embrace a larger context, even one inclusive of the New Testament, before the content of the Promise in the patriarchal stories is exhausted. The stretching out of the Promise is to be correlated with the extension of the context. This is not to assert that the Old Testament is "Christian Scriptures" nor to say that the Old Testament exists only for the sake of the New Testament. The Old Testament is an end in itself, and it belongs to Israel. What is now said is that the meaning of the Old Testament depends on the total context within which the meaning is sought. If this context includes the New Testament, Old Testament theolɔgy is oriented towards Christianity; if, instead, it includes the Talmud, Old Testament theology is oriented towards Judaism.

The second observation is about secularity. It might be alleged that when a secular theology is found in the Old Testament, the wish is father to the thought; secularity, it will be said, is a fashion in theology, and we are imposing our modernity on the Old Testament. It does not seem to me that this is so. This style of theological thought is really to be found in the Old Testament, but that is not to say that it is the only style of theological thought in the Old Testament. There is, so I would argue, a significant antimythological tendency in the Old Testament; antimythological in the sense that the world of Old Testament belief has been de-divinized. It is not a world which is alive with gods nor (in the kind of Old Testament theology which we are discussing) is it even one in which God makes special appearances. The reality of God is not dependent on theophanies, and in this world, where gods do not reside and do not appear, men are free and responsible and powerful.

It would be possible to show that even in the prophetic theology there is this secularity, and there is a sense in which Yahweh is hidden. All that there is on the surface is historical events, and the whole of history is made by man himself. All that there is to see is the efficient military machine of the Assyrians or the threat offered to Judah by the Babylonians. The prophets indeed say that it is Yahweh who is accomplishing judgment against his people, but Yahweh is not manifestly present in these events. Everything that happened to Samaria and Jerusalem is capable of satisfactory explanation without the hypothesis that Yahweh is punishing his people. It is explicable in terms of encounters between nations which have a normal political and military motivation. So there is a sense in which the God of the prophets is also a hidden God. At any rate, he does not interfere directly in human history. Neither the Assyrians nor the Babylonians are aware of his presence nor of any interdict on the exercise of their powers. They are allowed the full range of the powers of their humanity and nationhood, as are the Israelites and Judaeans in their political and military responses. It may be said that this is a one-sided account of the Old Testament, and this

I would readily grant. It is one aspect and no more, but there i
nothing scandalous in seizing on an aspect which seems to have
particular significance for our times, for this is one of the ways in
which the Old Testament can acquire a serious theological rel
evance. The use of the Old Testament as a "model" where it appear
to shed light on contemporary modes of inquiry is a legitimate ex
ercise of an Old Testament theology.

There is a theologically decisive difference between Gunkel and
von Rad. Von Rad's account of the theological enrichment of the
patriarchal stories by the Yahwist has nothing to do with the super
imposition of superior religious ideas. Von Rad has emphasized in
the first volume of his *Theologie* that an Old Testament theolog
cannot be constructed out of religious ideas or out of religious ex
perience.[9] This statement, for reasons which I have given, would
certainly seem to me to be correct in respect to religious ideas
Whether or not it is correct in respect to religious experience de
pends on what is intended by this elusive phrase. If what is intended
are particular forms of religiosity or types of piety, I would conclude
that von Rad's insights are sound in this case, too, for these canno
be "transmitted" and cannot therefore belong to an Old Testamen
theology. There is, however, a valid objection which may be raised
against the exclusion of religious experience, if its effect is to leave
us with a restrictive, kerygmatic theology as the only possible the
ology of the Old Testament.

It is difficult to determine whether or not this is von Rad's inten
tion. On the face of it, a theology which is dominated by basi
credal themes which are affirmations of "acts of God" is a restric
tive kerygmatic theology with an unanalyzed mythological content
Von Rad does not appear to take the matter further than this, but i
would be in keeping with the capacity for radical thinking which i
found elsewhere in his theology to refuse to be content with unan
alyzed "acts of God," to assert that this is credal discourse and no
historiography and that one should not understand it in such a wa
as to reinstate the supernatural in Old Testament theology. But i
these are credal statements which can have no theological rel
evance for us *qua* historiography, since they imply the invasion o

[9] *Old Testament Theology*, vol. 1, pp. 105 ff.

the supernatural into the historical order, we can only analyze them as affirmations of faith, and this means that we have reentered the sphere of religious experience in so far as faith is necessarily anthropological.

This is a central aspect of von Rad's theology which creates perplexity for us in our modernity, but which, nevertheless, releases Old Testament theology from any dependence on a normative body of religious ideas. The themes of Old Testament theology are not susceptible to any static, final exegesis. They take on new significance and make new demands again and again in relation to the changing context in which a faithful response is made to them. Old Testament theology has become an ongoing hermeneutical quest characterized at once by the continuity provided by credal themes and the initiative allowed to men of faith in every generation to discover anew what is entailed in a faithful response to the tradition.

Faith so conceived is not passive submission to a normative body of dogma. It is not a requirement that blinkers should be worn, that a deliberate narrowness should be cultivated, that the burden of intellectual inquiry should be laid down. It is a willingness to bear the whole weight of the burden of existence, to listen to all the voices that speak to our generation and to acknowledge the reality of the forces that threaten our authentic existence. It is to be open to all that is implied in being human in such a time as this and, out of the experience of being so exposed to the pressures and claims of our age, to discover that there is a tradition which can still be appropriated; that it is possible to rest on the grace of God. This believing is not a subscription to a fixed, objective body of dogma, but a way of life, a style of existence, a gladness in the givenness of the tradition, and yet an understanding that it does not exist independently of our faith. It is more than our faith, which is a response to what is already there, but it is a reality which is only actualized by faith.

4

Theology: Art or Science?

HARRY WARDLAW
Ormond College, Melbourne

There was a time in the history of the West, so we are told, when theology was regarded as the queen of the sciences. The theologians dreamed their dreams of making all of man's secular studies subject to this great sacred study which was seen as man's highest possibility. But Western culture has left such thinking a long way behind, and the theologians have been rudely awakened from their imperialistic dreaming. The secular sciences have long ago established their independence, and the independent work of natural scientists has been so impressive and so obviously fruitful that it would be foolhardy to challenge it.

Indeed, so positive, so persuasive, so assured have been the results achieved by natural scientists that their work is more and more taken as a model of what science can be and what it ought to be. It is natural science that seems to have taken us out of the realm of opinion and into the realm of truly scientific knowledge. Other approaches to reality seem to offer mere speculative fantasy in comparison with this impressive body of assured results.

Perhaps this growth in the prestige of natural science has been most marked in the empiricist atmosphere of Great Britain and the pragmatist atmosphere of North America, and in the English language the very word "science" has become more and more restricted in popular usage to mean simply the natural sciences. Furthermore, in many of the universities of the English-speaking world almost the whole field of human scholarship is divided into two parts, the sciences and the arts, and apart from faculties of professional training such as medicine, law, or architecture one finds two major faculties, one conferring degrees in science and the other in arts.

60

It would be wrong to make too much of this division of faculties, yet it may be taken as symbolic of a certain attitude of mind according to which the natural scientist is seen as the man who deals with the world of reality (for what is science but the knowledge of reality?), while all other intellectual pursuits are concerned with the world of the imagination (for what are the arts but expressions of the imagination?). Such an attitude would seem to leave the theologian with an embarrassing question: What is theology, an objective science or a subjective fantasy?

Theology, Science, and Imagination

The obvious way of disposing of the question is, of course, to show the inadequacy of this division of human thought. It is just not true to say that it is only the natural scientist who deals with reality, nor for that matter is it true to say that it is only the non-scientist, someone like the writer, who exercises his imagination. The work of the novelist or the poet may have a very obvious and significant relationship to reality, and the work of the scientist may display the most astonishing imaginative creativity. In fact, one eminent British scientist, Sir Peter Medawar, insists that "scientific theories . . . begin as imaginative constructions; they begin, if you like, as stories"; and from this he says "it follows that scientific and poetic or imaginative accounts of the world are not distinguishable in their origins. They start in parallel, but diverge from one another at some later stage. We all tell stories, but the stories differ in the purposes we expect them to fulfil and in the kinds of evaluation to which they are exposed."[1]

In view of this acknowledgment of the imaginative element in science and the realistic relevance of art one might conclude that the very division between realism and fantasy breaks down. And yet, while these considerations may certainly force us to restate the issue, I doubt if they really settle our problem completely. We cannot simply dissolve the differences between science and art as if they were of no consequence. It may be true that the artist and the sci-

[1] P. B. Medawar, "Science and Literature," Romanes Lecture, *Encounter* (January 1969), p. 20.

entist both tell stories, so to speak, but, as Medawar says, the stories are intended to fulfill very different purposes. In view of this we may restate our question and ask not whether theology is an objective science or a subjective fantasy, but, rather, what the imaginative constructions (the stories) of theology are about. What purpose are they intended to fulfill? Is the theologian developing theories in the manner of the scientist to tell us how the world works or, like the imaginative writer, is he expressing a personal response to the world? Or is he doing something different from either of these?

If we try to find an answer to these questions by looking at what theologians are actually doing and have done in the past then we have to admit that different theologians seem to be doing very different things. One would first have to take into account a certain kind of natural theology which does seem to be developing theories, or, perhaps better, a single theory, about the world. Such theological thinking starts with the actual facts of the world as they are given to us in experience and offers a theistic theory as a way of accounting for all this factual material.

At first glance this may seem to have a close affinity with the work of the natural scientist inasmuch as both scientist and natural theologian proceed by postulating general hypotheses to account for what they see. But if you ask Medawar's question, *what purpose are these hypotheses expected to fulfill and to what kinds of evaluation are they exposed?*, you immediately see that the cases are very different. In the case of natural science the theory is meant to give us information about how things happen in the world; indeed, it is usually meant to contribute to the development of a mathematical calculus which will enable us to plot the course of events. But it is by no means clear that the theistic theory has any such purpose in view. The divine hypothesis seems to arise only when our questions reach beyond the factual realm of events *in* the world. In a phrase of Wittgenstein, we might say that the theistic hypothesis arises when we consider not how the world is but that it is.

And if the purposes of these theories are different, so are the evaluations to which they are exposed. The scientist's theory is exposed to a process of carefully controlled observation and exact measurement or mathematical sampling, but one can apply no such tests to the theories of natural theology. Perhaps in the end the only ground of evaluation in natural theology is to be found in the fact that the theory seems convincing to the thinker himself. Whether this means that the evaluation depends on how far the theory is *imaginatively* satisfying, as with a poem, or in some sense *rationally* satisfying, as with an argument, is open to question, but it may be that in the final analysis "imaginatively satisfying" and "rationally satisfying" are not as different as they first appear.

Alongside, or perhaps over against, this program of natural theology one must consider the rather different case of revealed theology. Here the theologian does not proceed by postulating a theistic hypothesis about the world at all. He proceeds by accepting a theistic terminology as a mode of talking about certain movements and events within human history, most importantly, of course, those events associated with Jesus Christ: his life, his teaching, his death, and the sequel to his death in resurrection and Christian preaching. In this case we might say that the theologian does not proceed by constructing hypotheses or making up stories at all. His story is given to him. It is a story which is acted out in history, and his task is to rediscover that story in all its integrity.

Theology and History

This suggests that we might find a place for such a theology within the realm of historical studies. Whether or not this would establish the scientific character of theology might then become a matter of definition. In the broad division of academic studies into sciences and liberal arts, history is usually placed in the latter category, yet the phrase "historical science" is often used in discussion of modern historical method. But whether it be called a science or not, history does seem to offer a basis of empirically grounded objectivity. Historians may not be seeking for general historical laws like the laws of natural science, but they are seeking for knowledge and understanding of concrete events of the past. Historians may not be able to test their theories by setting up controlled experiments and making exact observations and measurements, but they do have to argue their case on the basis of concrete evidence, and the plausibility of the theory is directly dependent on the weight of the evidence. In fact, the historian could be compared to the advocate arguing a case in a court of law. Like the advocate, he calls his witnesses, offers his interpretation of the evidence and perhaps of the motives of the witnesses themselves, cross-examines hostile witnesses, listens to the arguments of various learned friends who offer contrary evidence or counter opinion, and so on.

But can the theology of revelation really be accommodated within this pattern of empirical argument? Such theology is certainly fundamentally concerned with historical events, especially those events in which Jesus was the central actor. Like the historian, this theologian wants to know why people acted as they did, to understand how they saw their world and how they thought about human life. He wants to understand what Jesus himself thought and felt about the world and how his actions, his teachings, and his death affected other people.

All of these concerns are quite simply historical, and they are obviously of real importance for a theology which is concerned about the revelation of God in Jesus Christ. Such a theology can hardly be indifferent to what actually happened in history. But we also noted earlier that the theology of revelation accepts a theistic terminology as a mode of talking about Jesus Christ. Can this be accommodated within the field of historical discussion? If the claim is simply that this terminology was of great significance for Jesus himself and was of great significance to his followers who became the first generation of Christians, then it would certainly be a straightforward historical claim. Obviously one cannot hope to explain the lives of the apostles and the growth of the early Church without bearing in mind that these men believed in God and interpreted the life of Jesus in terms of their religious belief. The theologian, of course, wants to go further than this. He wants to see Jesus in the same perspective as those first Christians saw him, and even more, he wants to present Jesus to his own century in that perspective. But even here he need not be going beyond the proper sphere of historical study. If the historian wants to understand the life of the early Church, he must certainly need to understand what it is to see Jesus as the Son of God. And if he wants to explain this development to

is contemporaries he must try to help them understand this vision
oo. But if he ends up *confessing* Jesus as the Son of God then he has
urely gone beyond the boundaries of ordinary historical discussion,
or this confession is not part of the historical reconstruction or the
ausal explanation of events. Nor is it subject to the process of eval-
ation on the basis of evidence. Of course, the action of God may
e postulated as a kind of super-cause and the progress of the
Church and the testimony of the faithful may be cited as evidence
f this super-cause. Confession is something different from such
heoretical postulation, however. It is a form of basic self-expression
ather than the formulation of a speculative hypothesis. It is not
 matter of judging the apostolic explanation to be the most plausi-
le. Confession is more basic and more immediate than that. It is
ore basic because it concerns the ultimate ground or foundation
f our engagement with life. It is more immediate because it is a re-
ponse to a direct challenge which is set before us.

Does this mean that when we make our confession of faith we
tep out of the realm of historical research into a totally different
ealm which is theology? Here we must proceed cautiously. Chris-
ian theology has always made much of its historical base, and with-
ut that base theology could hardly claim to be Christian at all. But
hat does it mean to say that Christian faith is historically based?
Iere we must look more closely at what is meant by faith.

It could be argued that the English word "faith" is an inadequate
ranslation of the New Testament Greek "*pistis*," for "*pistis*" is di-
ectly related to "believing" ("*pistevein*"), while "faith" suggests
rusting rather than believing. Typically we have faith in a person or
 cause, and this means quite simply that we trust the person or the
ause. But the disparity between the two words is not so great when
ne considers the kind of belief the New Testament writers had in
nind. For belief in Jesus Christ was no casual matter-of-fact belief;
t was a fundamental relationship of love and hope and loyalty. In
act, it was indistinguishable from the kind of trust suggested by the
Inglish word "faith." But one must go even further. This was not
ust one particular relationship of trust among others. This relation-
hip was the ground of all trust, of all loyalty, of man's whole rela-
ionship with his fellow men and with his world.

This is something Paul Tillich emphasizes when he defines faith as ultimate concern. Tillich does not simply mean that this faith though more important, is one concern along with all the others. He means it is the basis of all concern, of all seriousness, of our whole engagement with life. In the course of life we are taken up with a variety of different concerns of varying importance to us, but faith is not identifiable with any one of our loyalties or commitments, not even with our particular loyalty to the Church. The issue of faith concerns the final ground in which all our particular concerns in life are rooted.

Of course, this whole idea of ultimate concern is open to criticism very like the positivists' critique of metaphysics. Just as the positivist is critical of super-theories which try to go beyond the actual description of phenomena, so he may be critical of the quest for a super-concern which underlies the separate individual concerns of life. We simply are seriously concerned about certain things in life Why not accept that fact without becoming neurotically anxious about it? But just as the bewildering metaphysical question *why is there something and not nothing?* cannot always be silenced by positivistic strictures, so the bewildering personal question *why be serious about anything?* will not always be silenced by practical common sense. And, for some people at least, the integrity of personal life seems to depend on a fundamental context of concern underlying all the varied preoccupations of life.

Having thus made use of Tillich's definition of faith, let us now return to the contention that faith is historically based. In terms of our discussion so far we may interpret this as meaning that the ground of commitment, of serious engagement in life, is discovered in the setting of history. This is, of course, a claim made specifically about the faith of the Christian and need not be true of all faith. Life might find its ground in a timeless sense of obligation, an ultimate categorical imperative, which is quite independent of the actual course of events, though such an imperative could become destructive rather than creative should it become a sign of sheer demand, of judgment without grace. Or again life might find an ultimate ground in the sheer life process itself, though this life-force for many people may seem so shapeless as to be devoid of real significance. But Christian life finds its ground in the context of historical events. This is not peculiar to Christianity, of course. Marxists could say as much, as could some other non-Christian humanists. But for the Christian this historical setting is seen in a particular perspective centered in Jesus Christ, who is himself understood first against the background of the faith of Israel and then in the light of the faith of the Church.

And how does one come to see history in this perspective? It is certainly not on the grounds of historical evidence, not even where the evidence bears on the person of Jesus himself. For the Christian faith is not based simply upon an evaluation of the life and teaching of Jesus, no matter how admirable that may seem to be. There is an additional element which belongs to the generation of faith, an element of immediate challenge in the presence of the Gospel. For revelation, as Rudolf Bultmann insists, always belongs to man's present. It is an immediate arresting of the attention, a challenge which opens up a whole field of possibility and responsibility for purposeful engagement with life. This, I take it, is the kind of thing Carl von Weizsäcker is describing when he says he has been "hit by the Word of Christ," and he adds, "In a way this word has made life impossible to me; the life I might have lived without it has been destroyed by it. In a way it has made life possible to me; I am not certain whether I would have found a possible way of life without it at all."[2] This striking impact of the Word of Jesus has an immediacy which bypasses historical evaluations and reconstructions altogether. In a certain sense, the whole issue seems to narrow down to a point of bare imperative: "Follow me!" In a way, the immediacy of this call lifts it out of the arena of historical debate altogether. It is something which belongs to the present, not a view concerning the past. This is what makes the question of the historical Jesus so puzzling for Christians. If it were proved that Jesus had never lived, or that he was quite different from the figure in the Gospels, what then? This is a puzzling question for those who have been directly struck by the words of Jesus, because this striking figure who has arrested their lives is so bound up with historical origins that it seems

[2] C. F. von Weizsäcker, *The Relevance of Science* (New York: Harper, 1964), p. 77.

almost impossible to think of them apart. Yet honesty must surely forbid that we draw historical conclusions on the basis of such present experiences, no matter how vivid they may be. The imperative of the present moment is one thing, the weighing of evidence about the past is another.

However, the imperative of the call of Christ cannot really be separated from the teaching and the whole vision of life contained in the writings of the New Testament. This is all given together, and whatever the historical grounds of the New Testament documents may be they do supply the setting for our meeting with Jesus Christ. And this means we are called into a context of vision that puts history in a dramatic setting of evocative mythological imagery which goes far beyond the sober business of straightforward historical interpretation.

To talk in this way about evocative imagery suggests that theological study lies outside the realm of factual investigation altogether. It begins to look as if one is dealing with imaginative work such as one expects from poets, novelists, or playwrights. But perhaps one should say that the imaginative work has already been done and is contained, for the most part, in biblical writings and more particularly in the writings of the New Testament. Thus, it may seem that the theologian's job is not to produce the poetry of faith but, rather, to comment on a literature which has already been written. On this showing, theologians might be compared with the successive generations of literary critics who turn to the plays of Shakespeare to make ever new analyses of their imaginative form and content. In the case of the theologian, of course, the imaginative literature is kept alive in the preaching and sacramental enactments of the Church. But this too has its parallel in the case of the literary critic, for the plays of Shakespeare are also kept alive in ever new forms of production which bring them to expression for successive generations in classical or contemporary forms.

But can the Christian gospel really be compared in this way to a powerful piece of dramatic writing (or a group of dramatic writings grouped around a single theme)? Is there not a crucial difference inasmuch as the Gospel writers were responding to historical events in a way that William Shakespeare was not? When Shakespeare wrote the tragedy of Macbeth he probably cared little about that king of medieval Scotland, but when the early Christians wrote their Gospels they cared everything about Jesus Christ. And while the drama of Macbeth may show us something of fundamental importance about certain dimensions of human life, the authenticity of this revelation depends only marginally, if at all, on the historical figure of Macbeth. In the drama of salvation in Jesus Christ, however, the historical Jesus cannot be so easily ignored; for in this drama Jesus Christ has traditionally been seen not simply as illustrating the structure and dimensions of human life, but as the creative and effective source of man's salvation.

Here once again the theologian seems to be putting up something like a historical theory, yet a theory which really goes beyond the sphere of historical argument. To say that Jesus was the originator of the historical movement called Christianity or to say that he was the founder of that Christian community called the Church would be to make ordinary historical assertions, which are open to historical argument. But when we say he is the creative and effective source of man's salvation we seem to go beyond the boundaries of historical assertion. For "man's salvation" is not the kind of term that belongs to empirical historical analysis. And to speak of Jesus as the creative and effective source of salvation is not to speak the language of ordinary historical or social or psychological causality. One may, of course, attempt to discover the significance of the historical Jesus in terms of such social or psychological causality, and such attempts have been made. But, theologically speaking, they seem somehow to miss the heart of the matter. The theologian wants to go beyond this closed network of scientific and causal description. At this point, perhaps he will want to speak of divine creativity, a creativity out of nothing, which cannot be accommodated within a continuous nexus of cause and effect. But when such an appeal is made we have really left the field of empirical investigation altogether. The idea of divine creativity does not belong to the field of human explanations. It may be an effective way of drawing attention to the absolute character of the Gospel, but then it is just this absolute character which lies beyond the field of physical causal explanation. This does not mean we are dealing with something magical, like an event which has no cause. It means that we are no longer discussing historical causal explanation. Our explanations are applied to those things which lie *within* our field of interest, our engagement with the world. But the absolute, the Word of God, does not lie within that field; it serves to create it. It serves, as it were, to set the terms of all our interests and active engagements. It sets the terms in which we see the world rather than being one of the things we see.

Theology and Objectivity

What does it mean to see the world in this perspective? And does it have any connection with how the world actually is? I am reminded at this point of a photograph I was once shown of a landscape which consisted of strongly contrasting patches of white snow and bare black rock. When looked at in a particular way, these patches of light and shade could be seen to form a human face closely resembling traditional pictures of the face of Jesus. One might stare at the photograph for hours and not see the face, and some people could not see it even when the features were outlined. Yet when it had been seen, the impression was very striking. It was not just a matter of admitting that a certain area could, by a long stretch of the imagination, be taken for an ear or an eye; the photograph could be seen quite directly in its entirety as a picture of a face. There was a story told about this photograph, the details of which I have forgotten. The photograph was apparently taken by a man at some time of personal crisis, and the man's faith was renewed when he saw the face of his Lord unexpectedly looking at him from the landscape.

It is not hard to understand the impression such an experience might make on a man's imagination. There is nothing especially mysterious about this—astonishing perhaps, but not mysterious. The photograph can be shown and, in one sense at least, it is enough in itself to account for the man's excitement. But if someone asked whether it was really the face of Jesus the man saw or just the face of a local peasant who lived nearby, we might find it hard to know how we should answer. In one sense it was *really* deposits of photochem-cals on a piece of paper. In another sense it was *really* a photograph of a landscape. Beyond that, it was whatever it was seen to be, and if one man said "I saw the face of Jesus" while another said "I saw John the Baptist" or "one of the prophets," then all these reports might have to be accepted. But it is hard to see how one could speak of one way of seeing the picture as being right while all others are wrong (though some might seem obviously possible and others quite impossible). Is the position really any different in the case of a theology which sees a pattern of salvation in history or the face of God in Jesus Christ? Can the theologian have any real assurance that this is the right way of seeing history or Jesus? Indeed, does it make any sense to speak of such a way of seeing being right or wrong?

Perhaps as long as Christianity does open up an effective ground of ultimate concern, the sense of rightness is given within life itself. In such a case, it may be that the rightness of the picture cannot be challenged without challenging the very ground of the Christian's personal existence. But this makes the rightness of the picture relative to the lives of particular persons, even though it may be absolute within the terms of such lives. This, I take it, is what Karl Jaspers has in mind when he speaks of truth which is absolute but not universal. It is absolute for the life that is based upon it, but it is not one truth among others to be demonstrated, argued, and proved.

At first sight, this would appear to make one's fundamental life commitment impervious to all discussion and might seem to make creative theological dialogue almost impossible. But I do not think Jasper's view need lead to such negative conclusions. Men of faith may join in dialogue with each other whether they share a common vision or have quite different visions. And the ground of faith may be modified or even entirely undermined in such a dialogue. But inasmuch as the dialogue concerns personal absolutes, there is a sense in which a whole personality, a whole life-style, is being exposed, and such dialogue will not have the character of an objective discussion of matters of fact.

But if we abandon all objective points of reference in our discussions of response and commitment, are we not left at the mercy of mere personal whims? The German philosopher von Rintelen expresses some such fear when he is protesting against the restriction of words like "objectivity" to the sphere of corporeal entities. "If we eliminate these words from the human intellectual sphere," he writes, "its bases of meaning with their own proper order will almost be abandoned and will easily dissolve in the stream of subjective movements." [3] But to this one may surely reply that providing there *are* bases of meaning in the human intellectual sphere then these bases are themselves the ground of our discussion. One does not need to appeal to objective realities outside the human sphere, for the basis of discussion is given in human existence itself. But if on the other hand no such bases are recognized the appeal to external realities and authorities would be of no avail.

Has our analysis now gone as far as it can? Must we rest content with an account of theology which relates it to the fixing and expressing of personal absolutes, or must we not take a further step and relate the whole discussion to the objective reality of God? In most theological discussion it seems as if the reality of God is taken for granted. God is spoken of as the creative source or ground of the world, as the historic word of salvation, and as immediate spiritual presence. These three ideas are held together in an essential unity. And if one asks how one is assured of this unity, perhaps the only answer is that the unity is discovered in the context of the Christian vision itself. Thus, it is often said that the very idea of God is given in revelation; that is to say, it is part of that visionary context within which the Christian takes his stand. But can this language of faith be related to the language of objective fact, and, if so, how is it to be done?

Tillich has attempted to answer this question in terms of symbolism. The language of faith, he insists, is symbolic, as against the language of objective fact, which is conceptual. When we make our affirmations of faith, then, we are using a series of symbols which may be imaginatively very rich and suggestive but which do not have the same kind of literal factual reference which belongs to the conceptual language of descriptive science. But this does not mean that the symbols have no relation to reality. In fact, Tillich seems to sug-

[3] J. von Rintelen, *Beyond Existentialism* (London: Allen and Unwin, 1961), p. 88.

est that symbols relate us to reality more intimately than concepts, or while concepts may relate us to reality in a cognitive rational manner, symbols relate us to reality in active engagement. This distinction between concept and symbol may be quite manageable providing we can switch from the symbolic to the cognitive mode f speaking when we want to explain what we are talking about. But when we come to the confession of God, conceptual cognition becomes impossible, and only the symbolic expression of our engagement remains. But are we then engaging with anything? It seems as f this question cannot even be asked. One could only echo the often quoted words of Wittgenstein's *Tractatus*: "There is indeed the inexpressible. This *shows* itself";[4] though where Wittgenstein added it is the mystical" Tillich might have said it is the ground of being.

But whether the idea of the inexpressible really gets us any nearer o the order of factual assertion is open to question, for it has a certain self-defeating character, as Tillich himself seems to have recognized. So he suggests that the man who talks about "God" is in a real sense trying to do the impossible: he is attempting to represent what is beyond representation, beyond the conceptual sphere. Whether Tillich's idea of symbolism can really forge an effective link between the language of faith and the language of objective reality thus remains questionable.

A rather different proposal is made by T. F. Torrance, who rejects Tillich's idea of symbol and replaces it with the idea of an open concept. It is not always easy to distinguish between what Tillich means by symbols and what Torrance means by open concepts, but for Torrance the difference is crucial. Tillich leaves us with certain facts and imaginative constructs which are not to be identified with the divine but which do both point us to and relate us to the divine, while Torrance wants to go beyond these facts and constructs and conceive God directly. This is possible, Torrance believes, because God has actually given himself as an object of cognition. This is not o say that God is an object within the field of sense perception, but hen there is more to experience than sense perception. And Torrance holds that we will not reach a satisfactory cognitive knowledge

---

[4] Ludwig Wittgenstein, *Tractatus Logico-Philosophicus*, Second Impression (London: Routledge and Kegan Paul, 1933), p. 6.522.

of God unless we can break free from "the tyrannical assumptio
that all knowledge must ultimately rest upon a form of sens
perception." This "tyrannical assumption," Torrance holds, is r
flected in our continual use of the language of seeing. If we wer
prepared to use the language of hearing, however, we might find ne
possibilities of knowledge opened to us.[5]

This appeal to hearing I find difficult to understand. On the fac
of it, it simply means moving from one form of sense perception t
another. But perhaps the point is that hearing is more immediatel
related to conceptual thinking than is seeing. We hear words spoke
before we see them written. But how objects are presented to th
consciousness in hearing other than through the physical sense c
hearing, I do not understand. One might suggest that ideas presen
themselves directly to the mind, but to claim that such ideas shoul
be accepted as objects would be a very bold claim. Perhaps there i
more in this position than I can see, but I doubt if it succeeds an
better than Tillich's proposal in relating the language of faith to th
language of objective reality.

But even though this enigma remains unresolved, faith is nc
necessarily destroyed. One may still be left contemplating the visior
responding to the call to purposeful responsible life, and if in r
sponse one cries, "My Lord and my God!" perhaps this can onl
remain a cry, a confession, and a prayer.

It may now look as if we have dissolved theology and left onl
prayer, but this would be a premature conclusion. It does seem t
follow from what we have been saying that theology cannot claim t
be the "ology," the scientific understanding, of God, for God is no
given as an object of our understanding; "God" is the word we us
in our fundamental confession of faith.

But the theological task of outlining the shape, the terms, an
the symbols of faith remains. And we may still agree with Ronal
Gregor Smith when he says, "The basic question for theology i
neither What are we to do? nor How are we to think of things? bu
Whence do we receive?"[6] Whence do we receive the challenge t
serious purposeful living? This is where theology begins. But thi

[5] T. F. Torrance, *Theological Science* (London: Oxford, 1969).
[6] Ronald Gregor Smith, *The Free Man* (London: Collins, 1969), p. 28.

question is not to be answered by a rational exposition of the being of God. It is, rather, to be answered by exposing the roots of our faith. And if this faith is rooted in a historical context, then our theological reflection will unfold within that context, within a community and a tradition which is already given. Thus, the Christian theologian takes his stand within a tradition whch has already produced symbols, forms of confession, and authoritative writings. And while it would be a bad way of putting it to say this tradition provides the theologian with an *object* of study (as though his interest were merely anthropological), it does give him the terms of his theological reflection and perhaps even the rules of his theological discussion. Not that theological thinking can be confined by any rigid or unchanging system of rules. Quite clearly what is regarded as permissible in theology varies from one time to another and from one Christian community to another, and even the man who breaks the rules according to the Church of his own time does not cease to be a Christian and a theologian even though he be declared a heretic. The important thing is not that the theologian should agree with apostles, fathers, councils, popes, or reformers, but that he should listen to them and work in dialogue with them. And dialogue demands not only listening with respect but also answering critically. Of course the attempt has often been made to set actual limits within which theological thought must move if it is to be called Christian theology at all. But while such limits may be adopted as a matter of Church discipline it is hard to see how they can be said to define the boundaries of theology itself.[7] To argue about which theologians have the right to call themselves Christian is of little importance in the end. The importance of theological positions does not depend on the names they are given; the truth of theological positions is not established by Church decrees but by the living faith of persons and communities. And if this salt should lose its savor then authoritative pronouncements of orthodoxy would be empty and vain.

[7] Curiously, in our time it is sometimes secular philosophers rather than Church authorities who declare certain lines of thinking to be outside the Christian tradition. But perhaps the Christian tradition is broader and more accommodating than the critics allow.

5

History and Transcendence

IAIN NICOL
University of Glasgow

 T he one problem above all others which informs the work of Ronald Gregor Smith with unity and continuity is that of history and transcendence—how we may speak of their inter relationship in a dialogical way, and how we may do so without suc cumbing to the enticing theological cul-de-sacs where we are forced into a flat negation of the reality of one or the other. If we dare to take up this problem once again, it is in the hope that the following discussion may add something to the understanding of the problem and at the same time help to express a very sincere gratitude for the sensitive and profound insights which are part of Gregor Smith' legacy to theological scholarship.

The pivotal point for our reflections on the problem of history and transcendence is R. G. Collingwood's theory of historical under standing. Beginning with the distinction that he makes between the "outside" and the "inside" of historical events and understanding the outside and inside as interrelated in their compresence or coin cidence, we can see the sense in which history can be understood a the presence of the past. This can then be taken as a model for in terpreting the claim which inclusively transcends both past and present, the claim that Jesus is the Christ, *ho Eschatos*, the recogni tion of whom as such may be said to determine one's understanding and response to all other claims.[1]

---

[1] David Jenkins puts this similarly, "To discover that Jesus is the Christ is to discover the fact that is determinative of one's understanding of all other facts." *The Glory of Man* (London: Oxford, 1967), p. 37.

Theory of Historical Understanding

Collingwood's theory of historical understanding is well known nd does not require a lengthy exposition. However, the following passages from *The Idea of History* serve to focus our attention on he center around which his argument revolves as well as the central heme of this essay:

Historical knowledge is the knowledge of what mind has done in the ast, and at the same time it is the redoing of this, the perpetuation of ast acts in the present. . . . To the historian, the activities whose history e is studying are not spectacles to be watched, but experiences to be ved through in his own mind; they are objective, or known to him, only ecause they are also subjective, or activities of his own.

The historian, investigating any event in the past, makes a distinction etween what may be called the outside and the inside of an event. By he outside of the event I mean everything belonging to it which can be escribed in terms of bodies and their movements: the passage of Cae-ar, accompanied by certain men, across a river called the Rubicon at one ate. . . . By the inside of the event I mean that in it which can only be escribed in terms of thought: Caesar's defiance of Republican law. . . . he historian is never concerned with either of these to the exclusion f the other.[2]

A number of philosophical critics have taken exception to the heory of historical understanding suggested in these passages, and here can be little doubt that few contemporary philosophers would onsider it an essential or appropriate part of their avocation to de-end Collingwood's theory. The same can be said of some of the nore radically disposed theologians. For example, from the Form-Critical and post-Form-Critical theological perspective Colling-wood's views concerning history as the reenactment of past thought vould appear to be untenable, the nature of the Gospels being such hat despite every attempt to take them by violence, they refuse to

[2] R. G. Collingwood, *The Idea of History* (New York: Oxford, 1956), pp. 18, 213.

disclose the thoughts of Jesus, let alone permit us the luxury of re
thinking or reenacting them. In addition, the theologians who d
make this judgment appear to be able to make it without referenc
to the more agonizingly complex philosophical problem of othe
minds and knowledge of them.

Taken *au pied de la lettre*, it can certainly be shown that Colling
wood's theory is not only philosophically questionable at certai
vital points, but perhaps even theologically less fruitful than on
might at first have supposed. Nevertheless, if we consider the basi
distinction which he makes between outside and inside and the im
plications, if not the letter, of the spirit of this distinction, there ar
good grounds for assuming that his theory is still a valid and usefu
one when we recall that the wider issue with which Collingwood i
dealing is the problem of history as the presence of the past. And w
may suggest that within the context of this specific problem the ou
side/inside distinction is tenable and can be defended as being
useful description of what men actually do when they find them
selves confronted by a particular set of historical facts or by som
specific historical event. For instance, in a report dealing with th
assassination of a President of the United States or skirmishes o
the Sino-Soviet frontier, this outside/inside distinction provides
framework for asking questions such as *What is the Kremlin think
ing?* And, despite the fact that the answers to such questions ar
never readily available, men still persist in asking them in an attemp
to move from the external to the internal dimension of any event, or
in terms of Collingwood's theory, from the record of bare facts to th
thought and intentions of the agents involved. It can then be sug
gested that for historians, and equally for those who take an activ
and intelligent interest in either past or contemporary events an
affairs, the distinction may suggest something essential.

It is true that it is notoriously difficult to discover the motives o
thoughts behind historical actions not only because in most case
sufficient evidence is lacking, but also because historical agents fre
quently accomplish much more than they intended. But howeve
dubious such a pursuit may be, there is also a sense in which thos
who ask *What is behind this or that event?* may not in fact b
searching for demonstrable motives or intentions at all, but endeav

ring to discover some means by which a question-raising event may
be comprehended and explained in terms of the way in which those
to whom its question or questions are addressed understand them-
elves and their world, and in relation to their need to receive, give,
or even impose a meaning on that world. Therefore the outside/
inside distinction, though it may not be very precise or exhaustive,
is illuminating in this connection as a description of what as a matter of fact we do.

This, then, is to suggest that there are at least two ways in which
any historical event may be viewed. There is a "looking at" and a
"looking with." Understood in this sense, the distinction is not a
Manichaean one. It does not imply that there are two types of his-
ory, one of which is true and the other false. It does imply that
either can be entirely reduced to the terms of the other, or, as Col-
ingwood says, "The historian is never concerned with either of these
to the exclusion of the other." If for these reasons the distinction
may be defended and retained, the problem is now to discover the
dynamic connection between outside and inside in the historical
present, and to do so without being compelled to resort to a rather
artificial theological *duplex usus historiae*, which in practice frequently proves to be most useful to the theologian for its manifold
duplicity rather than its dialectical capacity.

At a quite fundamental level it might be asked why it is that certain historical events should concern us. A simple answer to this
question might be that the participation of any event in our present
is occasioned not only by the sort of questions we might want to
raise concerning any given event, but also by the kind of questions
such an event may raise for us. While it may be agreed that there is
always the possibility that any event whatever may have the power
to raise questions of a more ultimate nature, there are some events
which of themselves have the power to raise specifically ultimate
questions much more readily than others. For example, the life and
death of Jesus or Socrates are events which have the power to pose
and perhaps even impose questions about the ultimate nature of
things, their friendliness or meaningfulness. At the same time these
events may determine the way in which we speak about them. In
this sense, events such as these have something to say to the present.

However, as Collingwood suggests, before any event can brea silence and speak to the present, it has to be viewed in terms of it inside as well as its outside. To view the event from outside is to giv precedence to the more quantitative proportions of events such a times, dates, places, numbers, and movements, all of which can b calculated, recorded, compiled, and, if necessary, retold, and all o which can be established with a reasonable degree of accuracy. I addition to this, and to extend Collingwood's understanding of th outside of events, we might also say that in referring to the outsid of an event we are indicating, for one thing, the distance in tim which separates that event from the present and also the distanc and difference between the ways in which men in the past hav understood and expressed themselves in relation to their particula world and the events of their world. Certain past explanations o events are naturally quite strange to us since they presuppose a understanding of the world which we in the present can no longe wholly share. They have lost their immediacy and are no longer in tegral to the way in which we understand ourselves—in howeve fragmentary a fashion—and our own world. This, then, is to sugges that the outside of any event of the past is intensively bound up wit its "world," a historical, cultural, and metaphysical context or nexu in relation to which events have been grasped and understood an in terms of which they have been explained.

This last point provides an opportunity to mention one possibl misinterpretation of Collingwood's position. It is of particula significance with regard to those who wish to invoke his reference to reenactment to support the view that reenactment is essen tially an uncritical attempt to re-present the past in such a way a to neutralize its distance from the present and its strangeness. Th most obvious way in which this may appear to be accomplished is b means of an uncritical and self-abnegating identification, which despite the fact that the intention behind it may be to make the pas present and so rescue it and its values from the pit of oblivion, woul paradoxically appear to achieve precisely the opposite in that thos who put such a belief into practice tend to be rightly referred to a "living in the past." This is the past of spells and mystiques to whic the only attitude can be that of passive and reverent surrender. It i

he past in this sense which permits the eventfulness or happened-
ness of events to be submerged for the sake of that world in terms of
which they were objectively expressed, and which, with its insistence
upon the transposition or transference of the self into that past
world, must also demand a denial of the present.[3]

To return, however, to the more precise understanding of the
nature of past events and the sense in which these events are also
present, Collingwood is not so much criticizing this position as he is
he sufficiency of the subject/object scheme as historically applied,
and its alleged competence to solve this particular problem with the
somewhat *simpliste* assertions that history is an object to be con-
templated from a secure distance, that "facts speak for themselves,"
and that historical events can therefore be said to be present in
terms of a certain sum of firmly established and agreed facts about
them. And yet a further criticism which he wants to make in this
connection is one which concerns the ideal which the exponents of
his particular method strive to realize: that by means of the pains-
taking collection and arrangement of facts, any particular event or
series of events can in principle be reconstructed in such a way as
finally to constitute a self-explanatory unity. This is an ideal which
in turn implies that historical epochs, events, or any given series of
events, are, in principle, exhaustible; that the historical mine may be
abandoned when the deposits have eventually run out. Of course,
those who claim validity for this method would not deny that with
the emergence of fresh sources and data of other kinds, the historian
must always be under the obligation to revise his estimates. Nevertheless, this does not in any way affect the main thesis that, in principle, any given historical chapter can be closed and that there come
times when the prospector must move to more productive fields.

The historian of this particular methodological persuasion might
feel moved to protest that this description is really a caricature of his
position, and to support it further he may argue that the subject/
object framework is sufficiently flexible to permit a certain measure
of involvement with or sympathy towards the historical matter
which constitutes the object of his research. It is questionable, how-

[3] This is what Ronald Gregor Smith in a slightly different context has called
'the fallacy of immediacy." *Secular Christianity* (London: Collins, 1966), p. 79.

ever, whether it is really flexible enough. For even an involved or sympathetic subject would still appear to be the one who continues to control, determine, and even dominate. Thus, if the subject/object framework can justifiably be said to make any such concession at all, then the favor which it bestows accrues to the advantage of the subject alone, or, to adapt a statement of Hans-Georg Gadamer, history belongs to the subject, not the subject to history.

Despite these few but serious reservations concerning the adequacy of this method it is nevertheless necessary to emphasize again that there are few who would deny that there can be any genuine historical study without research into the outside of events. To ignore external history would be to place historical interpretation and understanding on a level with literary criticism, or, infinitely worse, it would be to reduce it to some kind of pneumatic vision, the primary concern of which would be to sever every contact with historical reality in its determined refusal to submit to any kind of empirical check.

On the other hand, however, it is not enough merely to establish the fact of the outside of any event, nor, in order to break the inflexibility of the subject/object frame of reference, is it sufficient to concede that in the light of new data and with the emergence of new sources, the historian must be engaged in a perpetual revision of his judgments. For what would count most decisively against this method is its insensitivity to the fact that historical events are not simply objects in the past, that they also have a future; that is to say, as raising questions or claims of one kind or another, they are already established and exist in a living connection with the historical present. Thus, any attempt to seal off the past, or any event of the past, as an object renders not only this living connection innocuous, but the past speechless.

Rudolf Bultmann, whose understanding of history in some ways resembles that of Collingwood, states this: "It is not at all 'in themselves', nor yet as links in a causal chain, that events and historical figures may be said to be historic (*geschichtliche*) phenomena. They are historic only in relation to their future, for which they have meaning and for which the present bears responsibility. It may therefore be said that to each historical phenomenon there belongs

own future, a future in which alone it shows itself for what it is."[4]
his suggestion would seem to be one which in practice Bultmann
mself has tended to disregard. Nevertheless, it does help to clarify
ollingwood's basic distinction between outside and inside, and
)es so also by attempting to overcome the more obviously idealist
)nnotations of Collingwood's own position. Thus, if the following
terpretation of Bultmann's statements is correct, and if a future is
tegral to every historical event to a greater or lesser extent, then it
ay be said that the past is not simply present as the possession of a
rtain aggregate of facts or information, nor perhaps even as a
teory or explanation of the past, and least of all as a pale reproduc-
on of history "as it really was." It is present, rather, as a claim
)on the present, and as a claim in which outside and inside are
sentially compresent or coincide. Therefore, as constitutive of
storical events, their future impinges upon the historical present
 this way, so that perhaps somewhat loosely speaking, historical
'ents can be said to possess an inherently "natural eschatology."

It has purposely been stated that a future is integral to historical
'ents to a greater or lesser extent. This is intended as a modification
 Bultmann's remarks, and it has also been stated specifically in
der to avoid the more luxuriant version of the idealist view put
rward by Croce, namely, that *all* history is present or contempo-
ry history, a view which, to its distinct advantage, would enable
im to speak of one kind of history and not two. By way of qualifi-
ition it may be pointed out that although the position being
gued for here comes close to this in many respects, it cannot be
id that all history is present history, though it may perhaps be so
)tentially or latently. This necessary qualification does not imply
iat a theory of two types of history has been surreptitiously rein-
oduced. It does mean, however, that events to which a future be-
ngs either latently or potentially are not thereby unhistorical, that
, on Croce's definition, not present, but they are of less value, in-
rest, or significance for our own history as selves or as persons.

Summarizing what has been argued thus far it can be said that we
innot cultivate a direct relation with the past in order to make it

---

[4] Rudolf Bultmann, *Glauben und Verstehen*, III (Tübingen: J.C.B. Mohr,

62), p. 113.

present. Nor, on the other hand, is the past simply present as a sol¹
and secure aggregate of facts. It is present, rather, as a claim or a
dress, and in this living connection of the past with the present, ou⁴
side and inside are apperceived as being compresent, and as beir
compresent to and with the *person* addressed.

History as the Presentness of the Past

As regards the question of the past and its claim upon or addre⁴
to the present and the structure of this particular situation, some ⁴
Collingwood's remarks again prove to be quite helpful. If the ta⁴
of the historian may be said to differ in any real sense from that ⁴
the archivist or the chronicler, then it must exceed the establis¹
ment, compilation, preservation, and transmission of facts, and tl
repetition of thought about thought about the past. Rather, Collin
wood writes, the "historian's thought must spring from the organ
unity of his total experience, and be a function of his entire perso
ality with its practical as well as its theoretical interests."⁵ And agai
in answer to the question What is history "for?" he says:

> ... history is "for" human self-knowledge. It is generally thought to ˡ
> of importance to man that he should know himself: where knowing hir
> self means knowing not his merely personal peculiarities, the things th
> distinguish him from other men, but his nature as man. Knowing you⁴
> self means knowing, first what it is to be a man; secondly knowing wh
> it is to be the kind of man you are; and thirdly, knowing what it is to ˡ
> the kind of man *you* are and nobody else is. Knowing yourself mea⁴
> knowing what you can do; and since nobody knows what he can do un⁴
> he tries, the only clue to what man can do is what man has done. Tł
> value of history, then, is that it teaches us what man has done, and th⁴
> what man is.⁶

At a superficial level it may look as though Collingwood is statir
something which may be painfully obvious to some historian
namely that history points morals, a view which for many others
just as obviously mistaken. At another level, however, what the⁴

⁵ *Idea of History*, p. 305.
⁶ Ibid., p. 10.

tatements seem to imply is that any claim or address which does
arise from the past to encounter the historical present is one which
s aimed not so much at making a quantitative increase of our knowledge about the past. Nor is such a claim or address to be regarded as
the external and static values which are to be understood as being
in some sense permanently appended to any given event, values
which may be repeatedly referred to as safe and dependable sources
of nourishment for the kind of practical wisdom which is a necessary
requirement for the conduct of everyday affairs. What Collingwood
seems to be suggesting, rather, is that such claims as do intrude
upon the present do so continually and in such a way that they can
never be wholly absorbed or exhausted in the present. Or, to para-
phrase the writer of James, they never simply become mirrors into
which a man may look and then immediately forget what manner of
man he was.[7] Such claims have a peculiarly persistent power to raise
continually and repeatedly a question or questions concerning the
manner of man he *is*, so that under the pressure of such claims and
because of the way in which they impose themselves upon the present, one is, in the light of them, required to reexamine and perhaps
revise and correct the way in which one understands one's life, or,
as Collingwood puts it, "one's entire personality with its practical as
well as its theoretical interests."

In *Wahrheit und Methode* Gadamer says that "Genuine historical (*historisches*) thinking must always operate in critical awareness of its own historicality (*Geschichtlichkeit*)."[8] If the interpretation of Collingwood given above is correct this statement of
Gadamer's provides a neat summary of his intention. At the same
time it throws into sharper relief the more implicit nerve of Collingwood's understanding of history, namely, that the reality of history
is essentially and vitally dialogical. The past may therefore be said
to be present to and with the historical present not simply as a
theory about it or an explanation of it. It is present, rather, as a claim
upon one's person, as an event constitutive of a total situation which
is irreducibly eventful. We may turn to Kierkegaard for an example

---

[7] James I: 23–24.
[8] Hans-Georg Gadamer, *Wahrheit und Methode* (Tübingen: J.C.B. Mohr, 1960), p. 283.

which is illustrative of the distinction between the kind of under standing and approach to history which permits such claims to arise and the kind which does not, between truth as "the way" and truth in the sense of a result. Kierkegaard writes:

There is a difference between truth and truths, and this difference is made especially evident by the definition of truth as being, or it is evident from the fact that a distinction is drawn between the "way" and the final decision, what is attained at the end, the "result." With respect to that sort of truth which permits a distinction between the way and the point ultimately reached by travelling along that way, the successor may find himself in a different position in comparison with the foregoer, he may be in a position to begin at a different point and slip into the truth more easily; in fine, the difference consists in the fact that the way is shortened, in certain cases indeed it is shortened to such a degree that it drops out, as it were, entirely. But when the truth is the way, when it is being the truth, when it is a life (and so it is Christ says of Himself, "I am the way, the truth and the life"), then no essential change is conceivable as between the foregoer and the successor.[9]

Kierkegaard then goes on to cite a number of examples, one of which is illustrative of the problem here under examination: "A man works laboriously to get an understanding of an obscure period of history upon which hitherto no investigation has been able to throw any light—finally, after spending twenty years on this work, he succeeds in bringing the historic truth to light and rendering it incontestable. The outcome inures to the advantage of the successor; the way is very considerably shortened, the successor requires perhaps barely three months to familiarise himself completely with the true situation in that obscure period."[10] The distinction which Kierkegaard is making is, of course, the celebrated one between the truths of history and the truths of existence, between that which can be objectively established and verified on the one hand and, on the other, the personal involvement of the subject. What he fails to

[9] Søren Kierkegaard, *Training in Christianity* (Princeton: Princeton University Press, 1941), p. 202.

[10] Ibid., pp. 203–204. The abyss may in fact be more narrow than one might have been inclined to suppose. See T. M. Knox's brief remarks in his Preface to *The Idea of History*, p. xvii.

emphasize is the fact that historical truth and existential truth cannot simply be left to go their own separate and predetermined ways, that they are not mutually exclusive but intimately and intensively bound up with one another at every point. Nevertheless, however exaggerated this particular distinction may be, and since for Kierkegaard distinctions of this kind inevitably must fall into the category of the "historical" and not the "existential" in any case, it is one which does in fact correspond very closely to Collingwood's distinction between outside and inside, and to his understanding of reenactment as these have been interpreted here.

Collingwood's distinction may therefore be interpreted to mean that there is a difference but not a dichotomy between outside and inside, that is, between the presentation of the facts and possibilities of a past historical event or situation in an objective way and actually living in those possibilities, or, as Ernst Fuchs puts it, "standing in the event." And if the interpretation of Collingwood's position up to this point has been a valid one, then the criticism which may with justification be made of Kierkegaard is not one to which he is open, since the outside of any event, which includes the objective establishment and description of the facts and the inherent possibilities of that event, is compresent with its inside as constituting a unitary moment with the self in the historical present. However, whether the problem of the meaning or significance of historical events on this view now becomes a matter of subjective inclination or taste rather than a matter of fact is a problem which must now be considered.

In order to distinguish the position which is being put forward from another one which is widely held and with which it may easily be confused, it may be added that the view of history which is being defended is not one which presupposes the specific theory of history as fact or event *plus* interpretation, as this is a view which would seem to suggest that the task of the perceiving subject is to go to work on the raw material of historical factuality in an attempt to superimpose an ordered interpretation upon it, and which, for all its apparent common sense, in fact reintroduces an extremely abrupt distinction between outside and inside as these are understood here. The virtue of this theory is the recognition that past events do not of themselves constitute the reality of history. On the other hand, however, that reality is not something which can be defined or described in this way, nor from the solitary perspective of an isolated subject.

In order to clarify this interpretation of Collingwood's view of history we may turn again to Gadamer. The situation which we are attempting to describe is one in which outside and inside cohere, are compresent as an address or as a claim upon the self. As such, it may be considered as a unitary situation in the sense that self and event stand together in dialogical reciprocity. Gadamer uses the term "*Horizontverschmelzung*," a melting of horizons, to describe this situation.[11] This term is intended to indicate that moment of historical understanding in which past and present coincide. With its suggestion of movement and change, it is also descriptive of the kind of situation of self with event in which one may apprehend in being apprehended, claimed, or addressed. To isolate the one from the other and place event over against self or self over against event, as a subject/object schema requires, would thus be to reduce what is basically a living and dynamic historical situation of essentially mutual reciprocity to a lifeless abstraction.

In summing up, we may say, first of all, that for events of the past to be present, no denial of the present or transference of the self into a world which is gone is involved. Nor are events of the past present purely in terms of a secure and precise aggregate of facts. An event is present, rather, as a claim or address to the self in a dialogical situation of compresence or coincidence, but not of identity.

The Historicity of Jesus the Christ

We must now go on to ask what relation this understanding of history may have with the things concerning Christ. Since this is not the place for an exhaustive survey, we may confine the discussion to a few observations. Collingwood's name has been closely linked with the New Quest of the Historical Jesus. It would seem, however, that having adopted a somewhat modified version of his theory of history as the presence or reenactment of the past, the New Questers have

[11] *Wahrheit und Methode*, pp. 286 ff., 356 ff. See also Carl Michalson, *The Hinge of History* (New York: 1959), pp. 27–28.

found themselves faced with some rather acute problems. One of these problems is that of the relationship between history and eternal happiness and the extent to which our certainty about the latter depends upon a decision concerning the former. One approach to this question has been to suggest that what is required is a decision about a past fact (Jesus' openness to transcendence), or, in similar terms, a decision on the basis of Jesus' own decision by means of which his certainty about transcendence somehow becomes our certainty. The difficulty of such a view is, however, that neither the nature and implications of Jesus' decision nor his openness to transcendence can be demonstrated with certainty. In this area, just as in others, we discover that history giveth, history taketh away. Or, as Van A. Harvey quite pointedly puts it: "No remote historical event —especially if assertions about it can solicit only a tentative assent —can, as such, be the basis of religious confidence about the present." [12]

If the source of our confidence about transcendence, the certainty that we are free or that life is worth living, is not to be located in an event stopped dead in its tracks in the past, where does it appear? In the view of history which has been outlined above we can say that it appears in the present constraint of a past event upon us in which outside and inside cohere and which has the nature of a disclosure. The disclosure is such that it has the power to illuminate our lives as a whole in the sense that such an event itself determines the way in which we speak about it and interpret it in its relation to other events, and the power to elicit our confidence, trust, and commitment.

Events of this kind may be called paradigmatic or formative events, whose *Sitz im Leben* is to be found as being intimately bound up with the story of a self or a community. They are not the kind of events which are consciously recollected in tranquillity nor made present by means of a strenuous exercise in the remembrance of things past. Their presence is primary. It is their dynamic and inexhaustible presence and its comprehensive relevance for the life of a person or a community with its hopes and fears and its sufferings

[12] Van A. Harvey, *The Historian and the Believer* (London: S.C.M. Press, 1967), p. 282.

and commitments which first sets in motion and indeed encourages not only that initial recollection but also, in the case of Christianity, ceaseless research into the problems and conditions of its historical origins, the quests for the historical Jesus, both old and new. As formative or paradigmatic, such events claim our recognition and response and invite our commitment. They do not present themselves only after having shed their more external proportions. Nevertheless, we are called upon to look upon them as imposing a claim or address; that is, to view them not so much in terms of their quantities but in the light of what they promise, and in the light of their respective abilities to lend our lives some coherence, meaning, and intelligibility.

There are many paradigms. They range from the typical gesture of the parent, which can become prototypical for the child, to the significance in the story of a nation of such events as the crossing of the Red Sea or the Russian Revolution. These are the kind of events which are constitutive of the identity of a person or a community—of the way they have come, the way they are and hope to be. They sum up their story, and in so doing act as a present point of reference and as the creative source from which selves and communities look backwards in remembrance and forward in hope.

The paradigm which refers to faith and to which faith refers is Jesus Christ. To quote H. Richard Niebuhr: "The special occasion to which we appeal in the Christian Church is called Jesus Christ, in whom we see the righteousness of God, his power and wisdom. But from that special occasion we also derive the concepts which make possible the elucidation of all the events of our history. Revelation means the intelligible event which makes all other events intelligible."[13] However, the recognition that Jesus is "the intelligible event which makes all other events intelligible," that he is the Christ, includes also the recognition that he is not just one paradigm among others. He is the last paradigm, *ho Eschatos*. And we have to say that such a recognition is not abruptly discontinuous with our recognition and response to the many other claims which arise to encounter us in our history. Christ is, in this same sense, present in the ongoing

[13] H. Richard Niebuhr, *The Meaning of Revelation* (New York: Harper, 1941), p. 93.

dialogue of history along with all the other claims which compete
for our recognition and allegiance, so there is no immediate difference between the way in which we can encounter his claim and the
claim or the address of any other historical event or person. If this
were not the case we would have to refuse the status of history to
every other claim and simply write them all off as part of a docetic
masquerade.

Yet at the same time there is a difference about this recognition
that Jesus is the Christ in that it really matters to us. While it does
not imply the flat negation of every other historical claim, it is nevertheless a recognition in which we do encounter him as *the* open
question to every other claim, so that the inevitable tendency of
these other claims to absolutize themselves is resisted and suspended
for the sake of freedom and openness. As *the* open question to history and to our own history, Christ goes before us sovereignly free of
the models we employ to describe him and of the propositions we use
often to circumscribe him. And it is in and through this freedom
that we are given freedom in and for history. It is the experience of
this freedom and the fact that it refers us continually to Christ
rather than back to ourselves that is the experience of transcendence. To alter very slightly a sentence from Gregor Smith's *The
Free Man*, we might therefore say that the transcendent is met in
the solicitude for history as given to us in the life and way of Jesus.[14]

---

[14] Ronald Gregor Smith, *The Free Man* (London: Collins, 1969), p. 100.

6

Kerygma: A Definition

DOUGLAS TEMPLETON
University of Edinburgh

The purpose of this essay is to clarify and explain a set, or what R. G. Collingwood called a "constellation," of absolute presuppositions, each of which is "consupponible" with all others. That is, it must be logically possible for a person who supposes any one of these presuppositions to suppose concurrently all the rest.[1] The presuppositions with which I am here concerned are, I suggest, the necessary ones for answering the question *What is kerygma?* My presuppositions differ from those of C. H. Dodd, Rudolf Bultmann, and Gerhard Ebeling, and I intend by implication to show the areas in which I disagree with these scholars in order to clarify what I understand kerygma to be.[2]

[1] Collingwood, *An Essay on Metaphysics* (Oxford: Clarendon Press, 1948) p. 66: "I speak of a set of absolute presuppositions, because if metaphysics is an historical science the things which it studies, namely absolute presuppositions are historical facts; and any one who is reasonably well acquainted with historical work knows that there is no such thing as an historical fact which is not at the same time a complex of historical facts. Such a complex of historical fact I call a 'constellation'." The relation between these "absolute presuppositions" is not (ibid., p. 67) "a relation of such a kind that a person supposing any one of them is logically committed to supposing all or indeed any of the others." But (ibid., p. 66) "since they are all suppositions, each must be *consupponible* with all the others; that is, it must be logically possible for a person who supposes any one of them to suppose concurrently all the rest."

[2] See C. H. Dodd, *The Apostolic Preaching and Its Developments* (London: Hodder and Stoughton, 1963). Also Rudolf Bultmann, *Das Verhältnis der urchristlichen Christusbotschaft zum historischen Jesus* (Heidelberg: Carl Winter, 1960), cited hereinafter as *SAH*. Also Gerhard Ebeling, *Theologie und Verkündigung* (Tübingen: J. C. B. Mohr, 1962). I disagree with these scholars as follows: (1) I disagree with Dodd on where he distinguishes history from eschatology. This disagreement would, I think, be supported by Bultmann. (2) I disagree with Bultmann by asserting Jesus' words to be *kerygma*. Dodd might be able to support this disagreement. (3) Although I have not undertaken any

Kerygma as Words Spoken by Christians

Kerygma is, at the least, words spoken. To say "words" is to exclude acts. However, the exclusion of acts is not an exclusion on principle but a methodological exclusion, since the question I am asking is not about pragma (act) but about kerygma. Kerygma and act can be distinguished but not separated. They must always occur together, as distinguishable aspects of one unity. And this unity I call "existence," the unity of word and act. If they do not occur together, then they are occurring as abstractions from the unity of existence.[3]

Kerygma, then, is words spoken and, more particularly, words spoken by Christians. The Christian man is one whose existence (words and acts) is qualified by the existence (words and acts) of Jesus of Nazareth in such a way that he is made free and responsible for others. To say "qualified" means that on every occasion he is the way he is because of a free and responsible relation to Jesus of Nazareth. And this relation is an historical relation of the same kind as a man's relation to Napoleon, the only difference being that the words and acts of Napoleon were the words and acts of God, but

---

criticism of Ebeling, as what he is trying to say and what I am trying to say is "post-Bultmannian," perhaps I may be allowed to say that I disagree with the prominence he gives to "the Word," which is a concept I do not follow, and refer, if I may, to Thomas Hobbes, *Leviathan*, edited by Michael Oakeshott (New York: Barnes and Noble, 1965), p. 39: "And therefore you shall hardly meet with a senseless and insignificant word, that is not made up of some Latin or Greek names. A Frenchman seldom hears our Saviour called by the name of *parole*, but by the name of *verbe* often; yet *verbe* and *parole* differ no more, but that one is Latin, the other French."

[3] I differ from Descartes's *Cogito ergo sum*. Cf. Ronald Gregor Smith, *J. G. Hamann* (London: Collins, 1960), p. 24. Cf. Søren Kierkegaard, *Concluding Unscientific Postscript* (Princeton: Princeton University Press, 1941), p. 302, cited in *Hamann*, p. 45: "The real action is not the external act, but an internal decision in which the individual puts an end to the mere possibility and identifies himself with the content of his thought in order to exist in it." Thus, *Sum ergo cogito*. See John Macmurray, *The Self as Agent* (London: Faber, 1957), passim: *Ago ergo cogito*. I am saying here *Ago et cogito: scilicet sum.* Gerhard Ebeling (*Luther, Einführung in sein Denken* [Tübingen: J.C.B. Mohr, 1964], p. 71) might imply something similar with his term *"Tatwort,"* but his emphasis is on the latter half of that word. Cf. ibid., p. 61: ". . . das . . . die *Reformation Sache allein des Wortes sei.*"

qualified by lack of freedom and responsibility. Qualified, if you must have it so, by sin.[4]

To say, then, that one is "qualified by Jesus of Nazareth" is to say that one is qualified by the man who is ascertained by historical science to have been, and to "have been for others."[5] That is, one is qualified both by the "mere that," that he existed, and "the mere how," how he existed for others. And "to exist for" is more precisely expressed in the categories of "freedom" and "responsibility." The obvious polarity of these two categories is then further heightened to the point of paradox by their equation; this responsibility *is* freedom.

The Christian man, qualified by the existence of Jesus of Nazareth, is free and responsible for others. But, for the Christian believer, talk of this relation to Jesus is in some sense also talk of God. By "God" I mean that which keeps me absolutely safe.[6] When the definition is introduced by a word no more pronominal than the word "that," I mean that if we go so far as to speak of God as a person, we have no real need to suppose that *in himself* he is such. Persons can, however, hardly go less far, just as no one would suppose the language of horses to be less than equine, or of oxen less than bovine—though for those horses that have experience of persons, it

[4] The doctrine of paradoxical identity (vide infra), that is, applies in both cases, but not in the same way.

[5] The phrase, of course, is Bonhoeffer's. His own words are *"Begegnung mit Jesus Christus. Erfahrung . . . dass Jesus nur 'für andere da ist?' Das Für-andere-da-sein Jesus ist die Transzendenzerfahrung!" Widerstand Ergebung* (München: Kaiser Verlag, 1951), p. 191. By science, I mean both the kind that is practiced by professors and the kind that is practiced by servant girls. Cf. *Concluding Unscientific Postscript*, p. 19. By "historical" is meant that history which is defined by Collingwood as the study of the actions of human beings in the past. Not that the theologian, of course, has an object of study that is different from the actions of human beings—in the past, if he is a biblical scholar or church historian; in the present, if he is a systematic theologian or dogmatist—but that the theological facts are not only historical facts and involve not only the risk of imaginative reconstruction, but also faith. (I allude to the "a priori imagination" discussed in *Essay on Metaphysics*, p. 241.)

[6] Derived from, of course, Wittgenstein (cited in Malcolm, *Wittgenstein: A Memoir* [London: Oxford University Press, 1962], p. 70n) though, no doubt, with what would be for him the multiplication of puzzling entities. Both Schubert Ogden, *The Reality of God*, (New York: Harper, 1966), and Van Harvey, *The Historian and the Believer* (London: S.C.M. Press, 1967), make some use of the saying.

)uld be nice to inquire whether their equipment would be suffi-
ent for them to speak of it.[7] God-talk, in short, is analogical. By
bsolutely safe" is meant, merely, that no thing in life, nor one's
aving of it, could make that safety insecure, though lest assertion
ould seem to run more than need be in advance of ignorance, the
st is silence. If what we know of life convinces us of God's care,
? may presume his sufficiency for what we do not know.

But what is the connection between this talk of God and what
as said of Jesus? If theological statements are, in Collingwood's
nse, "absolute presuppositions,"[8] that is, they do not depend on
1estions, but on them questions depend, then the question of the
anner of their relation is banned at the bar of the Spirit as a
eudo-metaphysical anathema. For we have arrived at the Chris-
in paradox and conclude with, or begin from, the belief, the fact,
e believed fact, the not-only-historical fact, *that* they are related.
he question "how" is solved and the Gordian knot is cut by prov-
g the question to be illusory.[9]

To suppose the paradox is to suppose that what Jesus did was
hat God did and that what Jesus said God said. By what Jesus did
.d said is meant his historical acts and words as ascertained by
storical science. And these historical activities of Jesus, his doing
.d speaking, at the same time as they are the historical activities of
man, are, to speak analogically, the historical activities of God,

[7] I refer to the fragment of Xenophanes, who remarks "that if horses could
flect on the semblance of the gods, they would portray them as horses." Cited
John Macquarrie, *Twentieth Century Religious Thought* (London: S.C.M.
ess, 1963), p. 57.
[8] For the equation of metaphysics and theology see *Essay on Metaphysics*,
10. Collingwood writes (paraphrasing Aristotle): "The ordinary name for
at which is the logical ground of everything else is God. The most adequate,
plicit, and easily intelligible name for the science which in its relation to other
iences is alternatively called First Science or Wisdom, the name which tells us
1at it is about, is therefore Theology." But it is also, by implication, his own
:w (see p. 46). Cf. *An Essay on Philosophical Method* (Oxford: Clarendon,
¡33), p. 126. For the doctrine of "absolute presuppositions," see *Essay on
etaphysics*, especially chapters 4 and 5.
[9] I begin, that is, by presupposing the relation between infinite and finite,
od and the world, God and Jesus. To debate whether that is, or is not, a datum
within theological discourse, a fallacy of misplaced argument. Cf. Dietrich
onhoeffer, *Wer ist und wer war Jesus Christus* (Hamburg: Furche-Verlag,
¡65).

who ate with men when Jesus did. What may be called the "*a alogia facti*" is to believe, or presuppose, that "the facts of the l and ministry of Jesus"[10] are the facts of God. I call this the doctri of paradoxical identity.

If the reader has followed all things closely till now, he will s that he has been engaged, on the one hand, in a narrative of thin that have been accomplished, and in a series of analogical assertio on the other. He has been asked to consider how it actually was a how what actually was, was God's history.[11] He has been asked remember the past, but not yet to remind himself that he, t exists in the present and faces a future.

Suppose, then, I say that I ask these questions of another, becau I must answer some questions of my own. I ask what he did, becau I am also asking what I must do. If I am interested in what I remer ber, I am also interested that it is I that am remembering. Suppos then, that the question I find myself having to answer is how I a to move out of my past into the future that is appropriate to me, how I am to make the future present. Thus formulated, the questic is general, structural, ontological; ontically, however, the questic will be defined by the situation in which I think I am standing.

If it is true that the question arises in the situation and if it true that situations are historical in the sense that present situatio are not exhaustively explained by the examination of past situatio if, that is, each situation is a new situation, then the question *wh did he do?* cannot answer for me the question *what must I do?* Nov if the past is "incapsulated"[12] in the present, there must have be a time when, in the first place, the past came to be. And things con

[10] *Apostolic Preaching*, p. 30.

[11] I have been persuaded by Ranke's famous phrase "*wie es eigentlich gewes ist*" to write "how it actually was . . . ," etc. To avoid confusion with the reje tion of the *Wie-Frage* above, it would be better if I explained that I mean this: "who, historically speaking, Jesus actually was and who, historically (th is, analogically), God was," or, in Collingwood's terms: "what Jesus did a what he meant by doing what he did and what God did . . . ," etc. But I do n mean that, despite what I said above, I am after all taking up the question *how God is related to Jesus*, though it is legitimate to inquire *what* it means assert that relation.

[12] Collingwood, *An Autobiography* (London: Oxford University Press, 193 p. 97, and vide supra.

o existence by being created. If my present is to come into exis-
ace, it must be created, and be created now, unless I recoil from
: task, or suppose there is none.[13]

Thus the whole inquiry till now has been a preliminary inquiry
ncerning an ancillary norm, namely, the historical Jesus, or, by the
ctrine of paradoxical identity, the historical God. But does he do
ything now? Whatever is replied to that question, at any rate by
ncillary norm" I mean that what he did offers me a criterion for
aat I must do, but a criterion that does not answer my questions.
r the questions for which what he did is a criterion are not the
estions I am asking. What he did is a norm, but it is an ancillary
rm.

And so, now that an answer has been suggested to the question of
dition and the scriptural and ecclesiastical past, the step is taken
o the axial phase of the three modes where the past is left behind
d a man presses forward into the arising situation, where the fu-
e becomes the present; because "for a man about to act, the
aation is his master, his oracle, his god."[14] For "History is now
d England" and now is the absolute moment.[15]

Something was said above, to speak analogically, of God the
ther, and something, to speak historically, of Joseph's son. But I
. now compelled to add the third, that is, to speak, and in tradi-
nal terms, of the Spirit, to speak, one must also say, of the
urch. It was also said above that the Christian man was qualified
the existence of Jesus of Nazareth. That is true, of course, but not
ectly true. More precisely, he is qualified by a discontinuous and
ntinuous succession of those who have been thus qualified. Nor
the *communio sanctorum* be circumvented by a searching of the
iptures, for to search them is to enter the community of those
o interpret them.

The doctrine of "paradoxical identity" is not merely a segment of
: history of dogma, but also a current dogma to explicate the ab-
ute moment. As a matter of past history, what those who have
n qualified by Jesus have said have been the words of God. And

---

[13] Respectively, the "antinomian" and "nomistic" error.
[14] Collingwood, *The Idea of History* (London: Oxford, 1956), p. 316.
[15] T. S. Eliot, *Four Quartets* (London: Faber, 1944), p. 43.

so, too, what Christians say, if at the same time what they s
is qualified by sin, as what Jesus said was not. Thus, not only is
true that what Jesus did and said was what God did and said, bu
is also true that what I do and say is what God does and says. Or,
short, with the qualification of sin, the doctrine of paradoxi
identity applies now as then.

Thus I—yet not I but the Spirit, regulated by tradition but r
confined by it—answer with freedom and responsibility, in so far
I assume or receive the questions that the situation poses, questic
that arise from but do not repeat the questions that were asked
the past, but to which, by dialogue, I answer with the greater w
dom. But lest the preaching of the Baptist should seem to suppl:
the place of Jesus, or Gospel be subordinate to Law, all does r
depend on how I answer, on whether I fly from the question or de
there is one, but on the belief, or presupposition, that whethe
answer or no, my safety is not touched. Demand and gift rema
but the greater is gift.

The presuppositions that have now been expounded have be
found necessary to explain what is meant by saying that kerygma
what Christians say. And these presuppositions are involved r
only in talk of Jesus or God or the Spirit, but in all that a Christi
says, even if they are, for the most part, no more than implicit. I
if it is these presuppositions that are being presupposed, then, i
suggested, the theologies of Dodd and Bultmann are vulnerable
places.

Kerygma and the Resurrection

In the first place, to take the question of kerygma and the resurr
tion, if the kerygma involves, on the one hand, historical stateme
and, on the other, what I call "the *analogia facti*" or theologi
statements, then it is important that the historical stateme
should be really historical. And that is important if Christian t
ology is to win emancipation from a metaphysics of "the st
says . . ." and move to a metaphysics of "history says . . . ," or, in ot

erms, from a faith that is mythological to a faith that is historical.[16]

That is not, of course, to say that a metaphysics of the story is bad metaphysics; it is only to say that such metaphysics is untimely when most people have given up that kind of thinking and do not have the time, and often the equipment, to immerse themselves in another age in order to understand the presuppositions of others far removed, which are neither their own nor need be. If servant girls do not at any time take kindly to metaphysical analysis, it is still more unkind to burden them with two, their own and others', than saddle them with one.

The notion of the resurrection belongs to that complex of notions called apocalyptic eschatology. All these notions suppose that history will have an end. But the notion that history will have an end is scarcely one that the historian can countenance. Nor, I would further suppose, need it be a notion which the theologian must accept. It is true, of course, that the personal history of the historian, as of all men, will, sooner or later, come to an end in death. But death ceases to be a problem if one believes, or supposes, that as far as what we know is concerned God keeps us safe, so that, accordingly, those questions that we have no means of answering, if there are any questions to be answered, may be entrusted to God's economy. That, whether I survive the ending of my life lies entirely in his hands, not mine.

As far as the resurrection in the New Testament is concerned, the evidence at our disposal obliges us to conclude that" Jesus died and that his followers, after his death, went on doing the kind of things he had done. So much for the "outside" of their actions. As for the "inside,"[17] the early Christians made use of the only metaphysical tools they possesssed. In the terms of their mythology, whose rubric is "the story says . . . ," they said that God had raised

---

[16] Cf. *Essay on Metaphysics*, p. 56. "History has its own rubric, namely, 'the evidence at our disposal obliges us to conclude that' such and such an event happened. What I call scissors-and-paste history has the rubric 'we are told that' such and such an event happened. There is also a rubric for use in narrating legends, which in some kinds of legendary literature is here and there explicitly inserted: 'the story says that . . . ,' or 'now the story goes on to say that . . .'."

[17] *Idea of History*, p. 213.

Jesus. However, in the terms of an historical metaphysics they would have outlined the "constellation" of presuppositions, which has been made explicit above. Or, if not these presuppositions, then something like them.

Kerygma and the Historical Jesus

In the second place, to take the question of the origin of the kerygma, we are supposing that what Jesus said was what God said and that what a Christian says is what God says;[18] and if what a Christian says is kerygma, then what Jesus said was kerygma. There is, however, undoubted discontinuity between what Jesus said and what the early Church said, if also continuity. But, one must also add, the relation of continuity and discontinuity between what Jesus said and what the early Church said is no different from the relation between any one kerygma and another, between, for example, the Palestinian Marēkyriology and the kyriology of Hellenistic Christianity. The question is whether the discontinuity between what Jesus said and what his followers said after his death is different in such a way that the term kerygma may not be used in connection with what he said at all. Jesus' message would then be not kerygma but its presupposition.[19]

The view I adopt here is to suppose that it was just as possible to become a Christian by hearing what Jesus said as by hearing what the early Church said.[20] The shift in what the early Church said away from what Jesus said, in so far as that is true, to "preaching the

[18] This is quite orthodox Bultmannian doctrine, e.g., *SAH*, p. 25 ff. In such a context it is Bultmann's wont to cite 2 Corinthians 5:18–20.

[19] Bultmann, *Theologie des Neuen Testaments* (Tübingen: J.C.B. Mohr, 1958), p. 1: "*Die Verkündigung Jesu gehört zu den Voraussetzungen der Theologie des NT und ist nicht ein Teil dieser selbst.*" In this quotation Jesus' preaching is, of course, one presupposition *among others*, as Jeremias points out. See Joachim Jeremias, *Das Problem des historischen Jesus* (Stuttgart: Calver Verlag, 1960), p. 11.

[20] Accordingly, I should wish to interpret John 5:24 ff. to refer also to the historical Jesus (though I do not, of course, suppose that these are *ipsissima verba*); whereas Bultmann writes: "*. . . es ist klar, dass Johannes nicht das Wort des historischen Jesus meint, sondern das Wort, das ihn Verkündigt.*" *SAH* p. 25.

reacher"[21] is explained in part by the fact that a man may not say
f himself what others may say of him, and in part by the fact that
ew historical circumstances necessitate new ways of talking. At one
oint Bultmann asks why the apostolic preaching is not content to
peat the preaching of Jesus.[22] But the history of Buddhism or
lato's treatment of Socrates or the development from Luther to
alvin or any movement of thought one cares to mention are in-
ances which suggest the contrary.

This is, of course, very far from suggesting that there was need to
orrect Jesus' teaching, but merely to say that no philosophy in
istory has eternal validity, for new situations, such as Jesus' death
the Gentile mission, demand that the new "strains"[23] be taken up
v a modified metaphysics; or, to put the same point in theological
rms, because the Spirit leads into all truth.[24] Thus, in answer to
ultmann's and Fuller's anxiety that "the effort to demonstrate the
ontinuity between Jesus and the Kerygma may so blur the differ-
ace between them, that in effect it will make Kerygma unneces-
ry,"[25] one must point out that not only did Jesus' message become
nnecessary to Paul and John but that the messages of Paul and
ohn themselves became unnecessary as they in turn were super-
ded by early Catholicism.

It should be further pointed out that if all history is present his-
ry, in the sense that it is now remembered, discussion of the pres-
atness of the past of which the kerygma speaks, in so far as it speaks
the past, is beside the point. The right question is not how the
Christ-event" is present, but who Christ is. And here Bultmann's
chotomy between Jesus the Jew and Jesus the Christ is false, for
either category applies.[26] Jesus was no Jew, in so far as, being the
essiah, he ended Judaism; nor was he a Christian, in so far as what

---

[21] A frequent formula of Bultmann, e.g., ibid., p. 17: ". . . *wie aus dem
erkündiger der Verkündigte wurde.*"

[22] Ibid., p. 23.

[23] *Essay on Metaphysics*, p. 48, Note to Chapter 5, and cf. pp. 74 ff.

[24] John 16:13.

[25] Reginald Fuller, *Anglican Theological Review*, 41 (1959), pp. 232–235
ited in Bultmann, SAH, p. 24).

[26] SAH, p. 8.

God said and did may be predicated of what he said and did in way that may be predicated of no other. For such a predication ma only be made of another, if it is made with the qualification intr duced by sin. In short, the kerygma of Jesus differs from the kerygm of the early Church in so far as the former is without that qualific tion. Any other differences are to be explained by the movement history, which the thought of men must move to meet or the Spir of God move over to pacify.[27]

In the third place, the New Testament critic is confronted by th phenomenon not of kerygma, but of kerygmata. Analogous pro lems occur, of course, in the field of church history; and the do matist, too, knows that others are declaring other dogmata. Th concentration, however, in this essay, is primarily on the New Test ment and the analogous situations are used merely for the purpos of allusion or illustration.

Kerygma and Kerygmata

What I wish to do at this point is to play off the factual historic insights of Ernst Käsemann and the theoretical insights of Colling wood against Dodd's theory of the development of the apostol preaching. Dodd speaks of one kerygma which is proclaimed i "fresh and invigorating forms." This is Dodd's synthetic approac or his unearthing of "the common faith" or "the fundamental Chri tian message."[28] But Käsemann would reply: "What commo faith?" In Käsemann's own words, "a theological problem is alread implicit in the fact that the canon presents us with four Gospels i stead of one and that even the first three reveal important dive gences in order, selection and presentation."[29] And, a little later i the same essay, he declares that the Gospels (to content ourselv with these), "take divergent roads. The pattern is as follows: Mar by means of his many miracle stories, depicts the secret epiphany him who receives his full glory at Easter, Matthew points to th

[27] I am thinking of Genesis 1:1 ff. and the "pacific" symbolism of the dov but not supposing that pacification is the only "work" of the Spirit.

[28] *Apostolic Preaching*, pp. 74–75.

[29] Ernst Käsemann, *Essays on New Testament Themes* (London: S.C.M Press, 1964), p. 95.

bringer of the Messianic Torah, John to the ever-present Christ, while Luke, historicizing and portraying salvation history as a process of development, composes the first 'Life of Jesus.' " And Käsemann concludes that "the question 'What is the Gospel?' cannot be settled by the historian according to the results of his investigations but only by the believer who is led by the Spirit and listens obediently to the Scripture." [30]

If one applies Collingwood's "logic of question and answer" and his theory of "historical process" [31] to what Käsemann is doing, and what Dodd has not done, then certain questions arise and certain answers may be attempted. First, let it be assumed that "a fresh and invigorating form" is not the "superstructure" on a "foundation," [32] but, to retain the metaphor, a new building, which, certainly, stands in an architectural tradition, but is not simply traditional. St. Paul's, in a word, is not simply the Parthenon built by an architect who did not know his job. As far as kerygma is concerned, a "fresh and invigorating form" is not a development or interpretation of the kerygma, but is kerygma *simpliciter*.

Second, let it be assumed, that no science may be said to deal with "eternal" problems, in the sense that all philosophers and all theologians have everywhere and always asked the same question and have given different answers. Let it be, on the contrary, assumed that, if different answers are given to the same question, then one or both are mistaken—and I ask, *en passant*, the question whether, at least in theology and religion, any one man, after careful analysis of his question, asks the same question as any other, and so whether contradiction occurs, though it is perhaps possible to say that one man may rightly evaluate his question as more important or relevant than the question of another.[33] And let it be further assumed that the correct answer to one question gives rise to new questions and that, therefore, a theology that is correct for one set of questions will

[30] Ibid., pp. 96, 106.
[31] *Autobiography*, pp. 29 ff., 97 ff.
[32] *Apostolic Preaching*, pp. 75, 10.
[33] Suppose, for example, that one man is asking a question about mission and another about ecumenism. It would still be possible for the first to assert that his question was the more important and so invite the other, not to ask the *same* question, but to ask *his own* question about mission.

scarcely be correct for the new questions which those answers raise

So much for the "logic of question and answer." When this logic is applied to the problems of kerygma, it is clear that there is no eternal kerygma, but a plurality of kerygmata proclaimed in a plurality of situations. Suppose that one kerygma conflicts, or appears to conflict, with another, then we must ask whether they are different answers to the same questions or different answers to different questions. Where they are different answers to different questions one must risk a judgment or be led by the Spirit or be confused by antichrist as to which is the right question to ask, and then as to whether the question one has chosen has been rightly answered. Where one judges, or is led to think, or is deceived to think, that correct answers have been given, one must go out after the new questions that now arise, even if one does not know whither one is going.[34]

Next arises the problem of what is called in theological circles "tradition" and of what is called by Collingwood "historical process." I quote him in extenso. He writes that:

. . . history is concerned not with "events" but with "processes": that "processes" are things which do not begin and end but turn into one another; and that if a process P_1 turns into a process P_2, there is no dividing line at which P_1 stops and P_2 begins; P_1 never stops, it goes on in the changed form P_2, and P_2 never begins, it has previously been going on in the earlier form P_1. There are in history no beginnings and no endings. History books begin and end, but the events they describe do not.

If P_1 has left traces of itself in P_2 so that an historian living in P_2 can discover by the interpretation of evidence that what is now P_2 was once P_1, it follows that the "traces" of P_1 in the present are not, so to speak the corpse of a dead P_1 but rather the real P_1 itself, living and active though incapsulated within the other form of itself P_2. And P_2 is not opaque, it is transparent, so that P_1 shines through it and their colour combine into one. Therefore, if the symbol P_1 stands for a characteristic of a certain historical period and the symbol P_2 for the corresponding but different (and therefore contradictory or incompatible) character

34 Hebrews 11:8.

istic of its successor, that successor is never characterized by P2 pure and simple, but always by a P2 tinged with a survival of P1.[35]

Mutatis mutandis for kerygma; it is plain that a man may find himself confronted by a new situation, by new questions, but he does not come to it destitute of what I call "ancillary norms." In Collingwood's terms, if he finds himself moving from P2 to P3, both P1 and P2 are there as ancillary norms to guide his steps. So much is transparent. But where the matter is not transparent is in the actual move from P2 to P3, which must be taken in the dark, where his only light will be his own judgment or God's.

The historical Jesus, to call him that, is just such an ancillary norm. But the present norm is the Christ of Faith, to call him that, or (which is the same thing) the Spirit. And, as who he is may not be known, a Christian must decide anew whenever a new question arises. And what a Christian then does is pragma, or not; and what a Christian then says is kerygma, or not.

These pages, though concise, must be concluded; but not without a word on their genesis. They took their origin in a persistent but incoherent dissatisfaction with what Dodd and Bultmann had said about kerygma. The problem was to express this dissatisfaction. And this could only be done by asking what I take kerygma to be and asking why Dodd and Bultmann should take it to be something else. And that could only be done by asking not only what kerygma is, but asking a great many other questions as well. What, in short, was involved was, willy-nilly, an essay in theological method.

If these speculations are tenable, they have implications for further criticisms of Dodd and Bultmann and almost certainly for other areas of theological concern. But to divide is to conquer; and the immediate problem was to examine what I took to be three central problems: the resurrection, the "historical Jesus," and the problem of the plurality of *Sprachereignise* to which that Jew or Christian gave rise.

Progress or clarity here might mean progress and illumination at other points as well. But only by making these presuppositions on

[35] *Autobiography*, pp. 97 ff.

what I take kerygma to be and by examining what they take kerygma to be was it possible to conclude with a definition and to know what was meant by it. Kerygma, then, is what a Christian says, if he has not been deceived by the father of lies;[36] and not only that, but, if he has been led by the Spirit, what God says, too.

---

[36] John 8:44.

7

A God I Can Talk To

A. D. GALLOWAY
University of Glasgow

Contemporary philosophy of religion has been obsessed with the question *How can we talk about God?* But for contemporary religion a more immediate and pressing question is *How can I talk to God?* The two questions are, of course, related. A God who cannot be spoken about cannot be known and therefore cannot be addressed. Yet there is an obvious sense in which God is not available to be known as objects of the world may be known.

Martin Buber, on the basis of his marvelously sensitive analysis of the I-Thou relationship, has argued the case for a God who can only be addressed but cannot be spoken about. I cannot imagine the case being better put. He has drawn attention to a decisive aspect of our relation to God with a clarity which is irresistible. But we are left with an inescapable and crippling problem. How can I address God without knowing something about him? I have to know and believe that he is the kind of being who can be addressed, that he has in some fashion, however preeminent, the characteristics of a person. In believing this and affirming such belief I must refer to him in the third person. This counterargument has been developed with relentless and compelling logic, particularly by Ronald Hepburn and H. D. Lewis.[1]

It is no solution to say that we are dealing here with a paradox. I would not deny that paradox is a legitimate constituent in religious and theological discourse. It is wrong to dismiss paradox as mere

---

[1] Ronald Hepburn, *Christianity and Paradox* (London: Watts, 1959), pp. 29 ff. H. D. Lewis, "The Elusive Self and the I-Thou Relation," *Talk of God; Royal Institute of Philosophy Lectures*, 2, 1967–68 (New York: Macmillan, 1969), pp. 168 ff.

contradiction and therefore uninformative. A contradiction be comes a paradox when both of the contradictory elements appear t be truths which we have good reason to affirm, but it still remains contradiction. A paradox may be informative in that it draws ou attention to and deepens our perception of the insights which driv us to make the contradictory assertions, but it does nothing to re solve the contradictions.

Certainly God is not an object like other objects in the world- not even the greatest.[2] The question *Do unicorns exist?*, thoug similar in its superficial grammar, is logically different from th question *Does God exist?* Anyone who expected the name "God" t appear in an inventory of all the items in the universe would be mi understanding the meaning of the word "God." God is certainly no available for our knowledge and inspection in that way. Anthony Flew appears to similarly misunderstand the logic of the wor "God" in the use he makes of John Wisdom's parable of the in visible gardener. The parable tells of a plot of land tended by a invisible, undetectable gardener. The parable attempts to show tha such a gardener, because he cannot be detected by any empirica test, is indistinguishable from an imaginary or nonexistent gar dener.[3] But has anyone ever believed that God is that *kind* of bein and that we could ever have that *kind* of information about him But despite his (possibly deliberate?) theological naïveté Flew ha made a valid and quite fundamental point. A God about whom w can make no valid assertions in the third person has died the deat of a thousand qualifications. He is a nonentity in every sense of th word. He does not even deserve the funeral orations of the death o God theologians. A thoroughly agnostic belief in God would b undistinguishable from a thoroughly agnostic disbelief. Neithe would involve any significant theological assertion or denial. W need to represent God to ourselves even to deny him.

[2] Paul Tillich, *Systematic Theology*, I (Chicago: University of Chicago Pres 1951), pp. 235 ff.
[3] Anthony Flew, "Theology and Falsification," *New Essays in Philosophica Theology*, ed. Anthony Flew and Alasdair MacIntyre (London: S.C.M. Pres 1955), pp. 96 ff.

God as Transcendent

Religion in general is a way of representing the gods to ourselves in order that we may present ourselves before them. In pagan religions the gods are characteristically available for representation. They are so bound up in natural elements that it is difficult to say whether these natural elements represent them or they represent the natural elements. They are available in cult objects. They are adequately represented in idols. But because of this, as the Scriptures of the Old Testament never tire of pointing out, they are limited. They are open to attack and violation. There is no security in them.

But the God of Israel, whom the prophets proclaim, is a God of absolute sovereignty. He cannot be threatened, and so there is security in him. The price of this, however, is that no image of him can be made. The explicit prohibition of the decalogue is against graven images. It might be thought that this represented merely a stage in the development of religion whereby unsophisticated physical images of God are prohibited but spiritual and mental images are still permitted. However, something more profound than this is proclaimed by the prophets. The God who is totally sovereign must be totally transcendent. Only at this price can we have a God who cannot be threatened. Only at this price can we have the hope of an unshakable salvation and security in him.

The corollary of this faith is the desacralization of the world. The God who is wholly transcendent is no longer in the rushing wind or in the terrible thunderstorm or in the lush return of foliage and fruit in the spring because he has been removed into a transcendent heaven—his own dwelling place. But how can we represent such a God to ourselves in order to present ourselves before him? Every image of him is forbidden. Every image of him can be formed by us only in terms of the categories, concepts, and structures of our world, and so denies his transcendence. Thus, a religious relation to him seems no longer possible.

Our age, having been reminded by Kierkegaard of this uncompromising aspect of biblical teaching, has seized upon it almost with delight, as though we enjoyed its astringency. It is as though we delighted in God's absence and took courage from our dereliction. Why should this be so at this particular time? The evidence was there facing our forefathers as much as it faces us. One needs to be no more than middle-aged to remember the time when it was not so. Between the wars, when Karl Barth forced our attention upon this astringent aspect of the biblical tradition, the response was one of shock and bewilderment. For Barth, this negative theology was only one aspect within the dialectic of a theology of positive revelation. A generation ago it was his positive theology of revelation which was widely acclaimed and accepted. The negativities of his theology were only unwillingly accepted in the face of a spirited rearguard action. Yet now, within the space of a mere decade or two, the whole situation is reversed. It is the negative movement of the dialectic of biblical revelation that is embraced with an almost masochistic eagerness in the death of God theologies, in religionless Christianity, secular Christianity, Christian atheism, and other forms of negative radicalism.

Why are so many joining almost gleefully in this riot of theological iconoclasm? The reasons and the motives are no doubt complex, but one stands out fairly clearly. The God who was being so lightly and almost gleefully rejected is a graven image. He is not a graven image made with hands. But just as the more primitive pagan chooses the best that he has, the finest woods, the most precious metals, the best of workmanship, in order to represent his God, so we, using the best that we know, our highest concepts of the good, the true, the righteous, the moral, put these together to make an image of a God. This God is in our own image, and we worship him. But such idols always tyrannize over the people who make them. Our God tyrannized over us, imposing the standards, the outlook, the values of a passing phase of culture upon our age. It is an enormous and a happy relief to be rid of him. We have most respectfully laid him to rest and rejoice in a new freedom of mind and spirit and purpose which is justly thought to be analogous to the release of the peoples of Canaan from the *ba'alim* of their agricultural society. It is analogous to the release of the Gentile people of the New Testament period from their many lords and gods. It is analogous to the release of the Jewish people of Palestine from the culturally determined God who tyrannized over them in the Law. To us, all things are lawful. The freedom thus gained is genuine Gospel freedom. This is a release as genuine as that of Martin Luther when he shook off the whole burden of medieval piety from his shoulders in the realization that salvation is by grace and faith alone.

This is a story which has been told often enough in the past decade. I believe it to be a valid account of one aspect of what has been happening to us spiritually. But there is another side to the story. What has been suggested in many of the theologies of the death of God is that it was no idol that died, but God himself—the true and the living God. His death was the death of Jesus Christ—the death which cleansed the world not only of demons who tyrannized over us but of God as well. Our forefathers have said that what God has cleansed may no more be called common or unclean. We have said that what God by his death has cleansed can no longer be called sacred. There is no sacred any more, only the secular. The world is thus placed wholly at our disposal.

I find it significant that in the age when the prophets of Israel proclaimed the death and the nonentity of every idolatrous object of worship, including idolatrous images of Yahweh himself, great social, cultural, and economic changes were afoot in the land. King David had established the control of Israel over the trading caravan routes. Solomon had taken this opportunity to build up a commercial economy in Israel. The laws of the ancient agricultural community were no longer relevant. The ethos of the old agricultural community was no longer apposite to the spirit of the people. A God who was near to Israel in the sacred soil of Canaan, in the harvest of the land, and in the blood of the people and who sanctified an ancient way of life had to be rejected in the name of a new culture and a new economy. A commercial world which is to be available for buying and selling must be desacralized. I find it significant that it was also at the time of a great expansion in Arab commercial activity that the prophetic protest of Mohammed began among trading Arabs like the *Quraysh* of Mecca. I find it further significant, as others have remarked before, that in the great rediscovery of the prophetic protest against cult which took place in the

Reformation there was a very firm correlation between the spread of these ideas and the spread of the new commerce. Is it not just possible that the new welcome being currently accorded to the purely negative moment of the prophetic message, the smashing of every positive image of God, the emphasis upon his absence from the world, the puritanical emphasis on his nonavailability for any form of cult, is as culturally conditioned and as rooted in a movement of the human rather than the divine spirit as any of its more cultic predecessors?

Our suspiciously facile acceptance of the absence of God from the world, either by death or by absolute transcendence, has coincided with our becoming self-conscious about the new urban and technological society. The God who isn't there—the God who is conspicuous by his absence—can become as much a projection of our own self-understanding and our own image of ourselves as the idol of any cult. Only an idol-God can be absent; for God, if there is a true God, is omnipresent. We have yet to find—perhaps some of us are already finding—that such an absent God can tyrannize over us just as effectively as an idol who was present at the altar. A God who is absent becomes by his very absence not less but more conspicuous and his tyranny over us the more impersonal and the more terrible in judgment and in scorn.

Tillich understood well the ambiguity of this kind of autonomous self-assertion against a God who has become heteronomous, who is absent from the world, and who rules it in judgment, negatively, from outside and beyond.[4] The judgment of a God who is absent from the world in death takes place within the world. Autonomy creates new heteronomous structures which assume demonic proportions. They are demonic in that they are superhuman in power and subpersonal in character. The creations of our science, our technology, and our urbanization already threaten us in this way. We stand in need of a new salvation from a new threat before which former images of salvation are irrelevant. This qualifies our delight in the new secularism and limits our enjoyment of our new freedom.

It is certain, however, that we cannot return to the God who now stands in a heteronomous relation to our new culture. It is certain

[4] *Systematic Theology*, pp. 81 ff., 147 ff.

too that we cannot halt the advance of the new technology. Who would wish to? But we must regard it more thoughtfully, soberly, and apprehensively, and our delight in the absence of God from our secular world is qualified by an accompanying sense of dereliction and anxiety. For us, the quest for a God to whom we can speak, to whom we can appeal, must begin again.

There is a third factor in the situation which must be distinguished from the other two. This is the philosophical factor. The God of traditional theism has suddenly toppled from his throne, it is alleged, because the metaphysics supporting this conception are no longer credible. This is another matter altogether. It is certainly related to but by no means identical with either the prophetic denial of every image of God or the cultural autonomy of the present age. There is a metaphysical crisis for theology at the present time, but this is by no means the first occasion on which such a breakdown in the metaphysical framework within which we express theistic belief has occurred, and it will not be the last. It will not be the last unless we accept the view of Auguste Comte that human understanding has passed through successive stages, each leaving the other irrevocably behind. In Comte's view there was first of all the religious, mythological, polytheistic phase. Second, there was the metaphysical phase. Third, there comes the scientific age, which replaces both its predecessors forever. The arguments in favor of such an evolutionary view of the development of human culture are far more deeply imbued with the spirit and the presuppositions of the nineteenth century than the metaphysical theology which it condemns. Comte's views are themselves an ideology with its own metaphysical and even mythological assumptions. But even if we were to accept them, it would be a gross error to assimilate this kind of ideology to the biblical critique of religious images and the prophetic protests against the available God. This would be a very odd sort of eclecticism. Yet this is precisely what seems to be happening when current antimetaphysical philosophies are claimed as allies by antitheistic theologies, and together they are hailed as man's coming-of-age in Christ.

A more sober and critical approach to this problem must begin by asking: Who is this God of traditional theism who is alleged to have toppled so suddenly from his throne? What is this traditional theism? As soon as one asks this question one realizes that what is called traditional theism exists only in caricature. Is it the theism of Tertullian or of St. Augustine or of St. Anselm or of St. Thomas or of Calvin or of Schleiermacher, and so on? They were all very different in the metaphysical infrastructure which they employed. Is only one of them to be selected as the official representative of traditional theism, or are they all somehow to be assimilated with one another in yet another feat of eclecticism? The fact is that there never has been such a thing as "traditional theism." In every age, Christians have tried to express the glory, the majesty, the power, the transcendence of God in the language and the metaphysical apparatus available to them. The form of the theistic image has changed with every change in the dominant metaphysical scheme. Every phase of culture enters upon its own hermeneutical confrontation with the Holy Scriptures. The scriptural tradition is the only constant in the situation. But the matter of Scripture becomes a living word only when interpreted by actual people in their own situation. Their metaphysics—the total frame of reference within which they interpret—is part of their situation. There is no revealed metaphysics. There is no single metaphysics of theism.

It is true of course that ecclesiastical authorities have from time to time attempted to canonize a particular philosophy. This was notably so in the case of Aquinas' employment of Aristotelian metaphysics. But the attempt to make this metaphysical system absolute is now recognized as a mistake even by most catholic theologians. It is true that our metaphysics, in the sense of a total picture of reality or frame of reference within which we interpret our experience, is at present in disarray. But this is a cultural and philosophical rather than a theological and religious problem. It does not appear to me to be essentially different from the problem that faced St. Augustine in the prevalent metaphysical skepticism of late Roman philosophy. He fell back upon the metaphysics of Plato in order to be able to talk about God, but he made a new thing out of Platonism and established the frame of reference within which the Middle Ages largely understood and interpreted its own experience. A similar crisis arose when Aristotelianism gained a new foothold in

Europe and at the time seemed to many to herald the end of "traditional theism." Aquinas, very much the modernist of his day, restated theism in terms of this new metaphysics. Descartes in his turn put the cat among the metaphysical pigeons yet again and the doctrine of God was stated again in terms of rationalism, then of idealism. This process of metaphysical revolution and counterrevolution has been going on from age to age. It is a problem which has again become acute in our time. But it is a serious error to assimilate this problem to that arising from the prophetic protest against every image of God.

One must not confuse contemporary intellectual bewilderment with the far more serious and permanent problem of the "infinite qualitative difference" which separates us from the only kind of God in whom we may have hope. We are inclined, I think, to overdramatize the critical issues of our own age. Each of the elements in the crisis has parallels in other ages. What is perhaps unique to our times is the coincidence of all these factors together. Born of our anxiety is the realization that only a God who transcends all our images of him can help. Born of a new scientific technology is the opinion that only a wholly secularized world can be technically managed. Born of the loss of our metaphysical frame of reference there is an inability to form any image of God even if we thought such an image were legitimate. These three factors add up to general dereliction. And it is dereliction! For this reason I entertain more regard for the forthright atheist who affirms his atheism in the spirit of stoical humanism than for the Christian who *lightheartedly* affirms that he can get along perfectly well without God. From this stricture I would, of course, exclude Dietrich Bonhoeffer and those like him who really did speak out at dereliction. One needs, I think, to be rather more adult in order to cry out, "My God, My God, why hast Thou forsaken me?" than the adolescent who is wholly content with his first taste of emancipation. I am content to be as adult as Martin Luther. Can one be more adult than he was when he exclaimed: "*Wie kriege ich einen gnädigen Gott?*"—"How can I get hold of a gracious God?" Luther's use of the crude verb *kriegen* appears to be deliberate. It suggests total availability. It suggests a God who is "to hand"—who can be laid hold of. Nothing less will suffice if anxiety and dereliction are to be overcome. Yet only a God who is wholly transcendent, so that he cannot be threatened, so that we cannot go behind him and doubt him, has the power to overcome anxiety.

God and the Realm of the Personal

This is the problem which has dominated twentieth-century theology. It underlies the crisis in the relations between linguistic philosophy and theology. It underlies the theology of crisis in Barth. It underlies Tillich's theology of Being Itself—the God beyond God. It underlies the split in process theology between God in his abstract being and God in his actuality. It was over this problem that Ronald Gregor Smith agonized in his last years. *"Wie kriege ich einen gnädigen Gott?"*—"How can I lay hold upon a gracious God?"

Any proposed solution which drives a wedge between God as he is in himself and God as he appears to us and makes himself available to us only exacerbates the problem. Behind the God we know there would always lurk the terrible shadow of this unknown God. Behind the face of God there is the faceless one. A faceless God is a monster. To be faceless, or to have a face which expresses nothing with which we can enter into human reciprocity, is a defining characteristic of a monster. In the imaginary fantasies which play a substitute role for mythology in our culture, "the monster" plays a significant part. From the creature of Mary Shelley's *Frankenstein* to the more contemporary "creature from outer space," their terror lies essentially in their faceless, impersonal "otherness." Such a being raised to the power of divinity is not merely neutral in his impersonal otherness, he is sheer horror. This is what lies behind the emotional violence with which Martin Luther refused to countenance any notion of God other than the God who is graciously available within the vulnerable flesh of Jesus Christ.

Tillich is himself too much a Lutheran to be unaware of this problem. He tries to overcome the split between the God who appears to us in correlation and the faceless God who is Being Itself by recourse to his doctrine of symbolic participation. True symbols, as distinct from arbitrary signs, he argues, participate in the reality to which they point. The living God, who is known to us and accessible for us in symbols drawn from the realm of personal life, participates in the reality of the truly ultimate—the God who is Being Itself.

I think that everyone who has understood what Tillich is trying to do here feels a keen sympathy with him. But the metaphor of "participation" is less illuminating and carries less power of conviction in these nominalistic times than it did in the days when Neo-Platonism retained at least a residual influence upon ways of thinking and speaking. Besides, the more seriously we take the notion of participation, the more it threatens the principle of individuality upon which all personal relation is based. Finally, Tillich's symbol "The New Being," in which these tensions of essence and existence, of participation and individuation are said to be overcome, has been even less successful. It has failed to meet Tillich's own criteria for a successful symbol. It has grasped no one in its symbolic power. It has merely kept at bay the problem which it was intended to solve. Nevertheless, Tillich has penetrated the problem for us. He has brought us to a threshold.

Barth has chosen the opposite tack. If we reject every notion of participation—every suggestion of *analogia entis*—and thus give the absolute sovereignty of God's transcendence free reign, then the problem disappears. By emphasizing the infinite qualitative difference and eliminating every element of availability in God, we leave him free to make himself available to us in his own way. It is in virtue of, not in spite of, his transcendence that he is able to bridge the gap which separates us from his otherness. Yet this is not an act of naked sovereignty. It is a gracious act which confers and establishes real partnership between man and God. This partnership is consummated and established forever in Jesus Christ.

This certainly seems to hold out the promise of an answer to the problem with which I began: How can I find a God I can talk to? But a deep sense of uneasiness remains. The ominous "No" of the early Barthian dialectic still hangs over the whole story like a shadow which not even the gracious eloquence of his later Christocentric doctrine can dispel. Is this monster of absolute transcendent otherness real? If not, why bring him into the story? If he is real, then what is his relation to the gracious God who consummates his inti-

mate association with common humanity in Jesus Christ? It is clear
of course, that Barth does not *intend* to have any truck with any no
tion of a faceless monster-God. He attempts to maintain the identity
of God as he is in and for himself with the personal God of revelation
by speaking of a "primary" objectivity of God as Trinitarian.[5]
Within God as he is in and for himself, Father, Son, and Holy
Spirit are to be thought of as maintaining a relation of personal
communion. But what has been called Barth's "positivism of rev
elation" leaves these images isolated in a realm of their own, dis-
sociated from our familiar experience of the personal. The only way
we can have a God who is wholly and consistently personal is if
we can identify his transcendence within the realm of the personal
as we come to understand it in our own experience.

There is initial encouragement for such a project in the fact that
the biblical tradition has no hesitation in speaking of God boldly
and consistently in personal images. It is surprising that a tradition
which is so forthright in its condemnation of every image of God
should itself be so free in its use of them. God has a face, eyes, ears,
hands. He comes, he goes, he acts, he listens, he speaks, he loves, he
hates, he laughs, he mourns. Both Barth and Tillich acknowledge
this and agree that any attenuation of these robust images in the interest of a fastidious intellectualism would betray a misunderstanding of their logic and of their power of communication.[6]

How can a tradition which sets its face so firmly against images of
God go on to employ images so boldly? It is possible because the
images are all consistently personal and every image of the personal
already contains within itself the implication that it is transcended
by what it represents or expresses. This arises out of our ordinary
inner-worldly experience of the personal. It occurs both in our
knowledge of ourselves and in our knowledge of others. Self-
knowledge is unique. I know myself as a subject of experience, not
by inference or observation, but in the bare fact of being that subject. Yet even in this situation of unqualified intimacy there is a

[5] Karl Barth, *Church Dogmatics*, II/1 (Edinburgh: T. & T. Clark, 1957),
pp. 16 ff.

[6] "Nothing is more inadequate and disgusting than the attempt to translate
the concrete symbols of the Bible into less concrete and less powerful symbols"
(*Systematic Theology*, p. 242).

sense in which I do not know myself. I transcend every image of myself that I make in self-understanding and self-interpretation. Here is a model of transcendence which lies within the doorstep of my own life. Here is a transcendence which is not impersonal or suprapersonal but is a constituent and central element within the personal. In our knowledge of other persons, the same recognition of transcendence is involved. I cannot know the other even in the enigmatic way I know myself. I can think of him and acknowledge him as a personal subject only by reference to my own experience of being a subject and my own self-understanding. I recognize in the other person a transcendence which has a double aspect. I understand it by analogy with my own inner experience of transcendence, and also by the transcendent inaccessibility of the other in his otherness from me.

There is more than an analogy between this inner-worldly transcendence in the realm of the personal and the transcendence of God. They are coincident, though not identical with one another. The attainment of any new level in knowing or loving God is always coincident with the attainment of a new level in self-understanding and in knowing and loving our neighbor. If this does not occur, then our new-found knowledge of God is either empty scholasticism or hypocrisy. On the other hand, though there is coincidence here, there is not identity. The basic error of much existentialist theology has been to mistake the *coincidence* of knowledge of God and self-understanding for identity. The basic error of much so-called secular theology has been to mistake the *coincidence* of knowledge and love of God with knowledge and love of the neighbor for identity.

In acknowledging himself as person a man acknowledges more than himself. In acknowledging his neighbor as person a man acknowledges more than his neighbor. He acknowledges the whole context in which the word "person" carries the load of meaning that it does. But what is this load of meaning which the word "person" carries? What is this context in which it bears such a meaning?

"Person" is a post-Christian word. This is true whether it is used by a Christian or a humanist. It has become part of the vocabulary of secular culture. But it has been informed by Christian theological tradition and was born out of the womb of Christian faith. Cultures not so influenced by the Christian tradition have their own—often noble and perceptive—concepts of the human individual. But they do not have the concept *person* as it arose within Christendom. Today, even when Christendom is in a serious state of disintegration, the concept *person* is one of its most lively survivals.

Even "person" is not itself a distinctly biblical word—though it has come to mean what it means through the biblical tradition. The biblical word is *neighbor*. This too is a word common to biblical and nonbiblical traditions. But its meaning within the biblical context is distinctive. It is distinctive because the covenant between God and man determines the covenant between man and man. The two commandments in the summary of the law—the first that "Thou shalt love the lord thy God with all thy heart and with all thy soul and with all thy mind," and the second, which is like it, "Thou shalt love thy neighbor as thyself"—are not two separate or separable items of legislation. They are two sides of a single command whose singleness corresponds to the unity and singularity of God. Loving God is never a distraction from loving my neighbor. Loving my neighbor is never a distraction from loving God. Here is the clue to where I can find a gracious God to whom I can talk. The meaning of the words "God" and "neighbor" within the tradition of the Christian faith mutually determine each other. God is the one who determines who is my neighbor and what it means for him to be my neighbor. My neighbor is the one who determines for me what it means to stand *coram deo*, before the face of God.

The Transcendence of God in History

But is this not double-talk? And when one eliminates the double-talk does what I am saying amount to any more than a simple identification of God with my neighbor and society? If so, can we not eliminate all talk of God and talk instead only of my neighbor and my responsibilities to him? Ludwig Feuerbach thought so and suggested a simple identity of God with the human species. Emile Durkheim, for different reasons, found a virtual identity of God with the social community. Auguste Comte proposed a religion of humanity. Many today pursue a parallel course in Christian theology.

They do so for reasons often similar to the lines along which I have been arguing. How does what I have been saying, in my search for a way of talking of God wholly within the realm of the personal, differ from this kind of reductionism, if at all? It is important not to be confused on this point, for the difference is total and absolute.

A reductionist identification of God with the human species or society does not give us a gracious God we can talk to. The "species" and "society" are even more faceless monsters than any impersonal creation of metaphysical theology. As Hobbes accurately perceived, they resemble the Leviathan of the great deep more than they resemble God. The notion of God—the living, gracious God of the biblical and catholic tradition—cannot be derived from the natural notion of society. Equally, the notions of "person" and "neighbor" as they are understood in that tradition cannot be derived from natural societal relations. If "God" is simply another name for society, then there is not even coincidence of knowledge of God and knowledge of neighbor, much less identity. On the contrary, there is in every society a tension between the unity and fixity of the social structure and the plurality and originality of neighborly action. Who should know that better than us—a generation as deeply involved, both in the East and in the West, in a titanic struggle with the social Leviathan.

This is the old problem of the One and the many. If it is not being thought out today (because we have failed to see both its relevance and its seriousness), it is being fought out with batons, stones, and tear gas. Where it is not thought out it *has* to be fought out, for it is a problem we cannot escape. To be committed to my neighbors, who are many, I must be committed also to whatever determines the context of our meeting and our neighborly relations, be it party, state, or God. This is the social meaning of the problem of the One and the many. If the One is a faceless Leviathan, then neighborly relations will always take place within a framework of alienation. This is the meaning of my search for a personal God. It is not a search for a cozy personal satisfaction. It is a social and moral necessity which I cannot escape.

The kind of thing that is nowadays rather patronizingly referred to as "traditional theology" at least gave a general shape to the problem. "Hear, O Israel," it is proclaimed, "the Lord our God is one Lord." Yet his people are numbered as the sands of the sea. How then can there be for us even the promise of a coincidence of our knowledge of our neighbor with whom we can speak and the God who is eternally one and by himself? For Christianity the problem has taken a Christological form. God is one and the children of God are many. But ultimately in faith we have only one neighbor. He is Jesus Christ. An essential part of what it means to call him the Christ is that he determines what it means for other men to be our neighbors. Whatever we do to one of the least of these we do to him. To receive Jesus as the Christ in faith is to believe at least this.

It is here—in this historic event which centers on Jesus Christ—that the coincidence of the knowledge of God, who is one, and my neighbors, who are many, has its origin. It is to him that we must look if we are to understand how there can be coincidence of knowledge of God and knowledge of neighbor—coincidence without identity. This is what "traditional" Christology is all about. The language in which we have traditionally described it is perhaps clumsy—two natures coincident in one person so that they are without separation and without division; but also without confusion and without change, so that each remains what it is. Thus, coincidence is not reduced to simple identity.

Jesus Christ is our neighbor and as such is one of the many. He is man. But he is also *anti pollōn*—he stands *for* the many. In faith, he becomes the ultimate and single claim upon our devotion. He determines the context within which we meet our neighbor. He unites the transcendence of God with the personal. In him, God has a face. He is a God I can talk to.

This is more than mythology. But it can become effective vision for us only as we get it into gear with our own life-situation. In the twentieth century, our immediate confrontation with the problem of the One and the many is, in the first instance, social rather than intellectual. Earlier, I said that in acknowledging himself as person a man acknowledges more than himself; in acknowledging his neighbor as person he acknowledges more than his neighbor. He acknowledges the whole context in which the word "person" carries the load of meaning that it does. This is the *"illud extra calvinisticum,"* the "something more" of God with which we have to reckon even after we have recognized him as our neighbor in Christ. He is the Father of the covenant, who determines the context within which we are persons in neighborly relation. Personal loyalty to my neighbor includes and depends upon loyalty to that context which transcends us both—even when my neighbor is Jesus Christ.

How do I combine the plurality of my loyalties to my neighbors with the singleheartedness of my devotion to that which makes them neighbors? This is the problem of the One and the many as it confronts us today. This was the problem in Prague when the most powerful element in the International Communist Party, claiming the right to determine the context of neighborliness, confronted the many with tanks in the streets. It was essentially the same problem at the Chicago convention, when the forces of law and order, representing the context of neighborly relations, came into conflict with the actual expression of neighborly concern. It is the problem at the heart of student confrontation with the forces of authority all the world over.

These conflicts are symptomatic. The first step towards seeing them in theological perspective is to recognize that the issues at stake are not essentially different from those of Nicea, Ephesus, and Chalcedon, where the doctrine of the relation of the One God to Christ our neighbor was hammered out. (That controversy too had a social as well as a doctrinal expression. The demonstrators were there in large numbers both within and without the building and came into violent conflict with both private and public police forces. The fighting at Ephesus was particularly severe and many heads were broken.) The question is ultimately this: Is the One who determines the context of our neighborly relations a faceless monster, a Leviathan with whom we must struggle in perpetual alienation, or may we hope in Jesus Christ for a God who may be known and adored with singleness of heart wholly within the realm of the personal? The choice is not between theism and atheism, between a living God and a dead God, but between God and Leviathan.

In all that I have said here, I have ignored the metaphysical problems which it certainly raises. I have confined myself to a kind of phenomenology of faith. I believe that we need a metaphysical structure in order to express more clearly what is here only vaguely hinted at. We may and we must, I believe, refurbish the theology of the ancient world. But we cannot refurbish the metaphysical terms in which it was couched. We do need a new metaphysics. A living metaphysics is one which formulates in the most general and abstract terms the concrete problems of the times. No such metaphysics is ever formulated in complete isolation from previous systems. Our age has already become sufficiently aware of the distinctiveness of its own problems—of its discontinuity from the theological past. The next step forward must be to see deeper into the real underlying continuity with our theological past. The central problem is still, as it always has been, *How can I lay hold of a gracious God?*

8

Theses for Understanding the Biblical Speech About God

HELMUT GOLLWITZER
Free University, Berlin

The Meaning of the Biblical Speech About God

1. Albert Camus says that the revolt "is only thinkable, after all, as directed against someone. Only the notion of the personal God who is the creator, and thus responsible for everything, makes man's protest meaningful. Hence we may say without any paradox that, in the Western world, the history of the revolt is inseparable from the history of Christianity."[1]

2. What contemporary atheism denies is the Christian confession of a "personal God" and the anthropological implications of this confession, especially the Christian speech about sin, and the Christian hope beyond death.

3. Thus, contemporary atheism is a phenomenon of that part of the world which has been shaped by historical Christianity. In other parts of the world this denial would be irrelevant. Wherever it takes its denial (e.g., in the form of Marxism) to other parts of the world (East Asia), it produces a relation to the world that has arisen out of Christianity: the de-divinized world as an object of profane science; the autonomy of man, e.g., his responsibility for the world; equal rights for all men; the changeability of society.

4. The term "personal God" is open to thorough misunderstanding and needs clarification. Denial without clarification is the general defect of contemporary atheism, but it has the merit of forcing Christian theology to bring about such clarification.

[1] Albert Camus, *Der Mensch in der Revolte*, p. 33. Translated from *L'homme révolté* (Paris: 1951).

5. The misunderstanding created by the term "personal God" consists in the opinion that it describes God as analogous to human persons, that it conceives "God" as a kind of enlarged man ruling the world, which is a polytheistic idea of God (Judeo-Christian monotheism in this case only differing from polytheism by a numeric reduction to one God, and by summarizing in one God the functions of a great many, without in principle giving up the polytheistic personifying of gods).

6. Originally, "God" is not a name but a predicate designing something superhuman, namely: a. superhuman forces and powers of various kinds, threatening as well as helpful ones (polytheistic); b. the ultimate ground of being (as in antique metaphysics); c. that which in each present addresses men "unconditionally" (Paul Tillich), which makes a final demand and gives a final meaning.

7. In the biblical sphere, this predicate "God" acquires the meaning of a singular and becomes a (ersatz) name for the voice whose first hearers and proclaimers are the prophets of Israel and Jesus of Nazareth, and whose name, in contrast to the names of other gods, is given as well as hidden. It is indicated by the tetragram J-H-W-H which in the Old Testament is interpreted as "I shall be there (for you)." (Cf. Exodus 3:14–15 in Martin Buber's translation of the Bible.)

8. For the New Testament and the Christian community the speaking and the hearing of this voice happens in a pure and perfect way, and is valid for all men, in the person of Jesus of Nazareth. That is, Jesus of Nazareth is the ultimate word of this voice (John 1:1–18) *and*, at the same time, man hearing this voice and committing himself to it (as expressed in the Christology of the early Church with its formula "true God and true man").

9. This voice is also being heard in the witness of those whom it has touched (Israel, and the Church, in the confession of the community and of the individual). As the response of different historical people and groups of people to the one voice, the

witness itself is different according to the historical conditions, and it is defined as a witness by being an interpretation and a taking up of a position in confrontation with this one voice. The hearers of the voice will have to examine again and again whether the response is adequate.

>. While the voice is speaking, a communication happens (biblically, a covenant) between him who addresses and him who hears. Throughout the times, the hearers have understood themselves in a certain way through the enlightenment given in the address. They experience themselves within a new practice which is grounded in the acceptance of a friendship. The continuity of the community of this voice consists in this irreversible experience, in the accepting and the fresh doing.

1. This friendship and appointment to a fresh practice (Gospel and commandment) are being heard as unsurpassable, irrefutable, and imperturbable, e.g., as the ultimate ground of being turning towards men (Anselm: *id, quo majus cogitari nequit*): the ultimate ground of being speaks; the ultimate ground of being loves; the ultimate ground of being wills; the ultimate ground of being leads to a meaningful end—astonishing statements compared to anything religions and philosophies have ever dared to say about the ultimate.

2. So the ultimate ground of being enters into relation with the world and the individual, a relation which can be adequately expressed only in the language of personal relations between men, hence the anthropomorphic language of the Bible. It must be taken "verbally, not literally," which means that it has "to be taken verbally seriously as picture language, but not to be understood as non-picture language, that is, literally."[2] One partner in this relation is not another man but the ultimate ground of being entering into personal relation by the voice speaking; it is not one being in the world besides others, say, a polytheistically conceived God (cf. thesis no. 5), but *id, quo majus cogitari nequit*.

[2] Helmut Gollwitzer, *The Existence of God as Confessed by Faith* (Philadelphia: Westminster, 1965), p. 164.

13.   Why did we choose the phrase "ultimate ground of being"? ?
       derives from metaphysics, from philosophical theology; it
       meant when metaphysics use the term "God." It is the bound
       ary concept of any metaphysics when the question arises abou
       the ground of all beings. The hearers of the voice which :
       testified to by the biblical witnesses, by using the word "God
       for this voice, want to stress that here something speaks to me
       in a human way and turns towards men in a human way, som
       thing in which all beings are grounded and to which end a
       beings are and live, hence something to which all beings ow
       their existence.

14.   If that something to which all beings owe their existenc
       speaks to men in a human way and promises itself to men, the
       metaphysics' speaking of the ultimate ground of being canno
       be accepted: it is (originally) impersonal; it states the identit
       of beings and their ground, not the face to face of him who ac
       dresses and him who hears, of the lover and the beloved; i
       knows nothing of a turning towards men, of a promise, of a
       hope and a certainty. This is because, in answer to the question
       possible to men, philosophy formulates information possibl
       to men, whereas biblical faith formulates out of the contingen
       event of a hearing of the voice. This is not a matter of wha
       man can tell himself, but only of what he can be told (Kar
       Barth), which implies this sequence: first receiving, then doin
       (cf. thesis no. 9), first hearing, then thinking.

15.   This does not imply that philosophy and faith by necessit
       oppose one another; it only implies that philosophy canno
       afford the statements in which faith speaks of the ultimat
       ground of being, and hence cannot bear any responsibility fo
       them. The more obvious this difference becomes, the mor
       philosophy is being urged to keep asking questions and not tc
       establish itself as a doctrine of salvation, and the more readil
       theology will grant that its presupposition is not the self
       evident question about the transcendent, but the not self
       evident "inscendence," that is, the stepping into our history o
       "condescendence" and the coming down of the "transcen

dent" in the event of the ultimate ground of being turning towards us in the appearance of Jesus Christ.

6. The phrase "Word of God" used in the Bible and in Christian theology means that *we* (i.e., first of all, the people speaking it, Israel and the Christian community, but they are also representative of all men to whom they hand it on), through a voice speaking in a particular history, are confronted with a friend—with no less than the eternal ground of being as our friend. For Israel, this history is the history of the covenant of him who speaks both to and with Israel; for the Christian community, this history culminates and is concentrated in the history of Jesus of Nazareth in which the voice heard by Israel speaks the final word for all people. As it is the voice of the ultimate ground of being to which all beings owe their existence, it is called the Word of God, the Word of the Lord and Creator. As in this voice the loving kindness of the eternal ground of being makes itself known, the message mediating the hearing of this voice is called *evangelion*—the message or tidings of great joy.

> *Definition of the Central Terms of Thesis No. 16:*
> *A Voice Speaking in a Particular History Brings About*
> *a Confrontation with a Friend*

7. "*A friend*"
   a. Why do we choose this predicate which is not frequently used in the Bible (Exodus 33:11; John 15:14 ff.)? Because it indicates that, through hearing that voice, man's relation to the ultimate becomes positive, and this relation is the all-decisive basic relation of man. What we have to expect from the ultimate and finally decisive authority is not the indifference of a blind fate, not destruction in the abyss of nothingness, not the rejection by an inexorable court of justice, but everlasting friendship.
   b. This confidence is no more self-evident for the believer than for the outsider. It is only the voice speaking in a par-

ticular history which may provide the basis for making th
confidence possible. For this reason, the word "Lord"
the predicate of God which is most frequently used in th
Bible. In speaking of the Lord as a friend and of the frien
as the Lord, Christian faith implies: (1) that this messag
of friendship is not a matter of course, that it is a miracl
we receive life from where we might have expected d
struction; (2) that this message of friendship is certain c
victory: friendship being given by the ultimate authorit
cannot and will not be curtailed by other authorities, b
wins through as the ultimate reality.

c. Since the Lord declares himself our friend he can logicall
no longer be thought of as "the despotic God-hypostasis
which grudges man his autonomy (Ernst Bloch). Th
Lord as the friend implies: (1) he makes his power serv
his friendship; (2) he renounces any relationship based o
despotic commands and wishes to replace it by a partne
ship, that is, by the free response of the friend; (3) he doe
not grudge his friend's unfolding of all his possibilities an
attaining fulfillment and life but wants to assist him i
achieving it. The Lord as the friend then means that th
creator helps the creature to attain autonomy—*this* is th
dependence of the creature on the creator.

d. The confidence in the friendship of the ultimate authorit
which has been awakened by that voice is belied by th
appearances and hence represents a Nevertheless! *Neithe*
our observation of life, nor our scientific clarification o
the world, nor our metaphysical reflection and questionin
of our conscience tells us what that voice says. As th
ultimate reality they do not promise us eternity as ou
friend, but they show us the indifference of eternity, th
reign of death, the lostness of man in the universe, and th
impossibility of expiating our guilt. Thus, the proclama
tion of friendship is eschatological in a threefold sense
(1) by opposing the ultimate promise to the appearances
it declares these to be penultimate, preliminary, surpass
able, and thus the present time as the untruth; (2) by in

troducing friendship, the ultimate truth, into the present
time, the penultimate truth, it involves man who has been
accepted as the friend by the eternal friend in a struggle for
the intention of the friendship embracing all men against
the unreconciled present time; (3) this friendship is not
just verbal but real; it is the community of a *way*; it is the
company of the eternal friend in our temporal history; it is
the ultimate penetrating the penultimate; it is the participation of the creator in the history of his creature; it is
the presence of the eschaton on the way to the eschaton.

18. *"History"*

a. The everlasting content of that proclamation of friendship
is not an abstract which may be distilled from its historical
forms, but it happens in its historical shapes, namely as a
concrete "adjudication and claim" in every present between man and man, in every particular historical language, and, as such, critically related to particular social
conditions and historical events. This friendship is not
revealed in the form of a timeless doctrine but in the form
of history which is handed on by word of mouth.

b. The proclamation of friendship enters the contingency as
well as the continuity of history. The discontinuity of
contingency results in the speech about God transforming
itself (the Bible is proof of this, as it is a collection of
various kinds of speech about God dating from different
times and sometimes not agreeing with one another). The
continuity of tradition proves the permanence of the same
content: through the changing times, the same voice, the
same adjudication and claim calls out to the men who hear
the voice. Previous experiences are preserved for and in
later ones.

c. The historical events which are being related are not just
illustrations, nor are they to be seen on a level with natural
events. They are, rather, the history of the struggle between the hearers of the voice and their own disbelief, on
the one hand, and the disbelief of their contemporaries on

the other. Thus, in the changing situations, the voice itself struggles, suffers, is denied, succumbs, and triumphs.

d. In the history of Jesus Christ, the following becomes apparent for the disciples who recognize the truth of this history: (1) Not only the human speakers of that voice are concerned with what happened to it in that struggle so far, but the divine speaker himself is concerned. God himself shares the suffering in the history of man and of his messengers among men and in all that follows from it. (2) This suffering shared by God establishes the hope of history within the misery of history; it turns history towards hope. Such friendship is costly for him who gives it, and therefore turns away distress from him to whom it is given. Jesus' cross and resurrection are not merely an example, a symbol for the eternal friend's share and participation in the fate of his friends, but the basic realization of this participation itself. All further participation follows from it. This is what the New Testament wishes to express by concentrating on the history of Jesus. The salvation of all men (the eternal friendship with all men) is irrevocably connected with the particular history of this one man. (3) This history is also the participation of the eternal friend in the unaccomplished time: all history, as temporal history, is not yet finished. The friend's history with us is not finished. It has not yet reached its goal. But one thing in it has been determined, and this is the insolubility of the connection of the friend with his friends.

e. The history of Jesus and of those who are his (i.e., Israel and the disciples), which is being told, is a history of promise, that is, its telling is the mode of handing on the promise (*promissio*) to all men, which is grounded in the history of Jesus.

19. *"The Voice"*

a. The traditional phrase "the Word of God" has been replaced by the phrase "the voice": (1) to stress the quality of event; (2) to avoid the impression that we deal with a theoretical truth which may be encapsulated in a doctrine and handed on in tradition; (3) to indicate the unity of the friend's address throughout the various forms of its events in time.

b. For us, there is only this voice, which means there is no immediacy with God in the sense that God is immediately at hand for us. Therefore, we cannot make any statement about God. An "ontology of God" is not possible. We can only make statements about this voice, either historical or kerygmatic statements, which means either statements about the historical forms this voice takes when it is heard, about the human messengers and their particular message, or statements about our own hearing of the voice and our handing on its adjudication and claim; in short, about the "witness."

c. If we have God only through hearing the voice, and if we take the proclamation of friendship seriously, this implies both that God remains hidden in mystery, *and* that he abandons himself entirely to us. (1) God remains hidden in mystery, that is, his being remains incomprehensible for us. The voice imparts to us the being-for-us of his will. The Word of God is *promissio* (promise), not a theoretical information about the ultimate ground of being; it is promise and acceptance coming out of the dark (or out of a "light which no man can approach unto," 1 Timothy 6:16). (2) God abandons himself entirely to us; that is, in his twofold mediation through the voice (Word of God) and the men serving this voice (kerygma), he does not keep himself to himself, but the event of his "self-revelation" takes place. That is, we really experience the ultimate will of the ultimate ground of being. Through this mediation we are immediate to God and he to us.

o. *"Confrontation"*

a. We are confronted by a voice when it addresses us and we hear it. When this voice addressing us permeates our consciousness and thus our life, this is faith. Hence we do not "have" the faith, but faith happens in us through this voice addressing us and penetrating our life again and again.

b. Everything, then, depends on this confrontation happening and going on to happen. Faith is not grounded in itself but arises from hearing. Even where there is no event of faith, the confrontation is going on and, as such, is promise and hope for a fresh event of faith.

c. The confrontation with him whom biblical faith calls God does not happen in a direct way but is mediated through the Word of God. Thus faith is faith in this Word of God; it trusts it, rejoices in it, fears it, follows it. Wherever biblical Christian faith says "God," we may say instead "Word of God."

d. The confrontation with the Word of God does not happen directly, but through the mediation of the human word, of the "witness" of those who—again through the voice of other men—have been reached by the voice speaking the Word of God and have been moved to respond in faith. Whether the voice addressing us through the human witness meets us is always an open question. But it is an undeniable fact that we are always confronted by the human witness as long as there are people among us who testify to Christian faith. It is an integral part of the confidence of Christian faith that this witness and man's confrontation with it will never cease in all future times of man's history, throughout all the changes of civilization and social systems (*Confessio Augustana*, 1530, article 7 *perpetuo mansura ecclesia* = the Christian community which will be forever alive). In fact, this confrontation is a front-line position between that voice and ourselves who hear it. What with all our searching for God, it is not the God we have sought. He is different from the God we long for. This is apparent in the crucifixion of Christ, in which the "No" of all of us men to this God becomes manifest. The Christian message confronts us with a friend who seeks us even though we seek something other than him. Hence, under the impact of the confrontation that happens to us (*metanoia*), faith is changing our thinking from opposition to acceptance of this friendship.

e. People nowadays often ask about the experience which corresponds to the word "God." The place of this experience is no other than the confrontation described above. Here we experience the meeting with groups of people who have been reached by this voice and whose way of life has been changed by it. When we enter the new practice of living to which we are invited by the voice of eternal friendship beckoning us to the new society of the kingdom of God, we experience the promises and directions of this voice. We do not have these experiences first and, following them, enter the new practice of living, but they are its consequence. To have faith means, in following the hearing of the voice, to risk the new life to which it invites us.

9

Being of Age

Eberhard Bethge
Pastoral College of the Rhineland at Rengsdorf

It must be conceded that, in Germany, the word "*Mündigkeit*" (maturity or being of age) has become a worn-out slogan. This term is used to refer to religious, political, rational, sexual, or Christian maturity and provokes moralistic reactions. Conservatives speak of the decline of authority and of law and order; does anybody really wish, they say, for the coming of chaos? The pious wonder whether obedience is to be eliminated from the Christian vocabulary and the know-alls ask: where are they, the ones come of age? Who is of age? The slogan is worn-out because it promises what has not yet been realized. The giving and taking of maturity are unevenly distributed. Everyone claims something like maturity as his self-evident right. But is anyone willing to grant it to others? Has the Church taken the lead?

I find it disquieting that ecclesiastical circles in Germany are being more readily infected by disgust with the slogan than by a passion for what it portends. It is disquieting because once again Christians and humanists are deepening the ditch which separates their camps. Maturity is speedily becoming a concern for the humanist but not for the Christians. Twenty-five years ago it looked as if this ditch might be filled in. At the time of Hitler's dictatorship, when people were kept in tutelage, an amazing rapprochement developed between those who, amidst totalitarianism, actualized the freedom of the children of God and those enlightened humanists who had no longer expected very much from the hopelessly compromised Christianity. After 1945, however, those who had demonstrated their maturity in the previous period of totalitarianism were glorified, and their stouthearted action was understood and preserved as evidence

136

of obedience rather than freedom. Thus, the *Kirchenkampf* has always been interpreted and praised as a history of the obedience of faith and not as a struggle exemplary of man's coming of age. Had it been otherwise, the reconstruction of the Church, its teaching and its claims, would have looked different after 1945. Thus, the first impulses were allowed to die down, and others were left to deal with the theme of human rights.

Maturity and the Biblical Faith of the Reformation

Today the word "maturity" or "being of age" may be found in almost any issue of the Christian journals, but always as a slogan. That it is in reality so little accepted is shown by the fact that none of our Protestant German dictionaries of the last two decades has seen fit to record this catchword. We may look it up in legal dictionaries—but it does not seem to be a Protestant matter. There is a reason for this. Maturity has been handed down to us as a concern of the Enlightenment. But the Church considered the Enlightenment too rationalistic, too optimistic, and too rebellious. Furthermore, the Liberals, Socialists, and atheists were even more interested in man's being of age, and this disqualified it once again for the Christian consciousness. To Christian consciousness everything which was not based on the scheme of sin and grace and did not immediately fit into it remained suspect.

But in time people take what is not given to them. And now we are anxiously living through a period in which whole groups are taking by force what was withheld from them. Our society, our universities, our churches, our schools, even our clergy and our monasteries shake with the fever of an unsatisfied desire to make up for lost time.

My theme is that maturity and the struggle to be granted maturity are actually fruits of the Reformers' faith, and that means that it derives from biblical sources. It is in no way a concern of the Enlightenment alone. Why then have we allowed them to steal it from us? It is high time that we should become allies. Up until the present we have always criticized maturity from the outside. However, criticism is of no value in itself. A corrupt maturity has to be criticized for the sake of the better maturity.

This is only an assertion thus far. But who is able to hear it? Any one who at this point claims maturity as a fruit of the biblical faith of the Reformation must not forget that he faces a wall of skepticism. The Reformation's concern for man in the state of sin and grace has too acutely distrusted any concern for the human right of maturity. For too long we have discouraged rather than advocated emancipation. This wall of skepticism will not give way very quickly. Without any doubt the process of coming of age has also set in: in the planning of studies, in the ways of teaching and training, even in the way in which our ecclesiastical constitution and organization are being examined. But the way forward is a long one which will include many struggles over details, and unfortunately there is a lack of theologians and churchmen to give us courage and a good conscience.

Recently a German bishop wrote: "The central human problem appears not to be a society come of age but the salvation of man from death which is the wages of sin, his liberation from the law." Apparently, then, the Gospel of the salvation of man from death is not to be actualized as a society come of age. But what kind of "eternal salvation of man from the dead" could this be if it does not include God's adoption of his children come of age and also a concern for the adoption of others?

We have discovered how the painful, detailed, and hazardous commitment to a society come of age may be kept at bay. Some guardians of the Reformation call it Pelagianism, and that is always difficult to disprove. Other guardians of the Reformation say, "it is ideology-suspect." They continue, "We Christians of the Reformation know about sin." But who guards these guardians? Who watches over them to ensure that their criterion of sin does not become another ideology and another form of Pelagianism, that is, a pretext to leave things as they are?

Of course, sin and hubris will remain. But in this case sin and hubris consist of the rejection of maturity rather than of an impulse

[1] Bishop Heidland, *Pfarrerblatt*, 19 (October 1969), p. 614.

for it. The irrepressible desire to make men dependent, to cling to and fortify superiorities once gained—this is the first and foremost sin against God and man. He who denies maturity, not he who struggles for it, sins against the Gospel. If this is true and if the sequence in the catalog of sins is not turned the other way round, we shall not deny that a demonic obsession may attach itself even to our enthusiasm for maturity. But those who deny maturity are at least as guilty as the enthusiasts.

Since we are dealing here with objections from the Christian camp we should add a word about the theme of obedience, which is central to Christianity. None could deny its biblical reality or ignore Christ's fundamental obedience. But the mystery of this obedience is none other than the bringing about of this great freedom of maturity. Here the means and the end must not be exchanged. This is, in fact, the mystery of Christ, that for him obedience is, at the same time, freedom. In him, the one lives out of the other. Here the absolutely mature one addresses us.

It must also be said that we do not wish to deride the great tradition of the Fourth Commandment. There will still be punishment, commandment, and law, but surely they are not values in themselves. They have this one end: to make possible new free living-space. Commandments are the means, maturity is the end. In any case, the Gospel begins and ends at all the stages of necessary obedience by establishing maturity, and, biblically, this can be shown without difficulty.

In Genesis, man is called to shape his world on his own responsibility. The prophets struggle for costly freedom and against any form of cheap freedom. Jesus inveighs against the scribes who keep men in tutelage. He does not overrun his partner but creates a basis for him to be who he is. And the New Testament reaches its climax in freeing the community for the "adoption of sons come of age." (Galatians 4:5) In this chapter in Galatians the established social order of the time is called into question. In that order only he who was not born a slave might expect to become an heir come of age, who on his part again disposed freely of his heritage. In selecting the phrase, "adoption of sons," to describe Christians, St. Paul uses the conception of the most coveted legal and social status of his time. He writes: "God sent forth his son, . . . that we might receive the adoption of sons" (Galatians 4:4–5) and "ye have received the Spirit of adoption . . ." (Romans 8:15), which means the spirit of the free heirs who have been granted maturity.[2] The first and last concern of the Gospel is this adoption of free sons. It relates to obedience, redemption, salvation, and the kingdom of God whether now or at the end of all time.

In view of this we must ask whether it is possible that our bitter struggle against fanatics and enthusiasts has played us a trick, so that we are being taken for lawmongers, and nobody believes any more in our call for freedom. We say "Christ is our freedom," and the echo is heard, "repressive empty formula." All the same, Christ *is* our freedom, but such freedom is trustworthy only if we take sides with those who try to lead men forth from their immaturity. Man's maturity is always at stake.

Maturity as a Human Right

But what then is this maturity of which we speak? Is it adulthood? Who is able to have it? Do you have it once and for all? And what do we mean by Christian maturity? For teachers it is the purpose of education; for psychotherapists it is the guiding principle of therapy. For lawyers it means being legally qualified to transact business, to take an oath, to be married, or to be of the age of culpability. Their criterion is the dignity of man, which is guaranteed by his responsibility. This is actual and quite central and reaches far beyond the lawyers' offices and courts of trial.

In raising the question of the meaning of maturity we first asked if it meant adulthood. Christians frequently voice the opinion that man is not mature and proves daily how unfit he is to be of age. It is, of course, true that our society does not consist of Albert Schweitzers and Martin Bubers only. Adulthood and wisdom are good gifts of God but are rarely actualized. Maturity, however, is a human

---

[2] Luther's translation here speaks of a state "of children" and a "childlike spirit." This may be the reason why many cling to the unfortunate concept of the ideal Christian as a docile, obedient child that enjoys its dependence.

right, if not a legal right. As such, it is due to every person, however immature his behavior. It is therefore due to social and natural groups, to students, workers, and blacks, however threatening their behavior. Nobody is to withhold from man the state of self-responsibility or to take away from him his maturity. Everyone must have the right to make his own mistakes, although it is difficult for us, the older ones, to bear the burden of watching them made. Those exceptions who have the misfortune to be sick or mentally unbalanced make no difference here. On the contrary, these difficult boundary cases clamor all the more loudly for mature self-responsibility. And the Christian message of salvation with its hope for the kingdom includes them (with first priority) in the "adoption of sons."

Maturity thus understood as a human right and not as adulthood invalidates the reproach leveled against most concerns of the Enlightenment, that a naïve optimism of progress is being cherished. A claim such as this implies that maturity means that man is becoming better all the time. Certainly we should not give up hope that men and groups are becoming more adult all the time. But he who comes of age knows only too well how his delight in his freedom, won at last, and in his shaping of his own life exactly coincide with the burden of his full responsibility. We all know the flight from responsibility. Not everybody wants to be mature. It is far easier to let others decide and bear the responsibility. The strong man is wanted. Political parties make use of this desire for the father figure. It becomes ever more trying to find one's own place in the structure of powers and claims and social institutions. And probably one gets more deeply entangled in guilt because he stops enjoying his self in freedom. However, that does not exempt man from his duty and his capacity for an independent answer. It belongs to everyone.

We asked second: *Who is capable of maturity?* This question implies that at least two persons are needed in the matter of maturity, one who becomes mature in the process of his personal history and one who grants maturity—parents, institutions, or society. Maturity is really the opposite of individualism and unlimited self-determination. Maturity must not be identified with an unrestrained living-out of one's own desires. He who comes of age relates himself more and more consciously to his world and rightly expects his place in it to be acknowledged.

But conflicts arise at just this point. Probably we cannot avoid all of them, but might we not be able to limit them? They are difficult to avoid because a decision has to be made between a too early and a too late time for maturity. The declaration of maturity is not one which can be fixed for all times and all groups. An element of risk remains. Characteristically, parties and governments here and elsewhere debate the legal time of maturity and the right of voting. And here in Germany it is not the Church but the political left which has given the impetus. In most Western countries maturity has been granted at an earlier time than in Germany. But now changes are taking place here too which are partly due to insight and partly to the rebels.

In a county town the authorities have recently left it to the pupils of the last form to decide whether they want to attend school or not, to work or not. This would have been unthinkable in my own schooldays in the most Prussian part of Prussia. This courageous step has brought about a change in the pupils' sense of responsibility. Problems of discipline have suddenly become redundant. The majority of schoolmasters and pupils have asked for the experiment to be continued. Wonders have been worked, not by demanding adulthood but by a bold and unconditional granting of maturity.

Psychology helps us to recognize how vital it is to risk awarding certain rights of maturity early so that man may realize himself and continue to grow. According to Mitscherlich, "The individual can achieve independence only if he knows himself to be securely supported by the sympathy and goodwill of his neighbors in his first attempts to exercise his initiative." "Safely supported"—that is what matters. If there is no goodwill, there is less self-realization. If maturity is withheld for too long, destructive rebellions may be the consequence.

In the case of the individual, he and those related to him pay the cost if a rebellion cannot be avoided. In the case of groups, which are in the process of self-realization, the whole society pays the cost if maturity is not granted. We are experiencing this in the workers' struggles for partnership and in the unrest within the universities and the synods of the Church. Of course we must be careful not to oversimplify things. These anxious processes of self-realization contain a mixture of genuine concern for partnership and unallayed motives of power and self-interest. The more this is so, the more severe are the forms which the struggle takes, and the more difficult it is to decide the proper time for maturity, the too early or the too late.

In granting political maturity to the Congolese, the Belgians provide a frightening example of irresponsibility in poor preparation. The history of Black Power in the United States probably proves what happens when maturity is granted too late. The aid to development will be doomed if, however much shot through with self-interest, it will in the last resort not promote maturity in those who receive it. That is, there must be a granting of their own responsibility and education for a political, economic, and cultural self-determination. There will never be a process of maturity unallayed by power politics. It is no use waiting for it. But any solidifying of the guardian's rights in the political, economic, and cultural field will prove to be a source of ever new catastrophes.

And what about the Church? Once she proclaimed Luther's "priesthood of all believers." Once the Reformed Church struggled for and won the sovereignty of the local congregation over against the centralized power of the whole Church. But it is her role as a guardian which has become actualized in her one-man system and in her talking down to the people. To abandon this role is more difficult for her than for any other existing institution. Of course, some changes in the organization may be made here and there. Thus we are discussing the proper age for baptism, the admission to communion, the age of election to her different bodies, the rules which restrict persons to a particular parish, and the reexamination of the article on heresy. But even here little will be changed unless real pressure is brought to bear. In the missions field two great wars were needed to make us grant independence to the black churches.

There are however deeper reasons for the hesitation of the Church. In the course of the self-liberation of Western man from ecclesiastical guardianship, the process of secularization in philosophy, science, and morality has called into question all traditional conceptions of the Church: the conception of God the Father, of the Lordship of Christ and his apostles, of obedience, and the authority of ecclesiastical proclamations. The crisis is a profound one, and it is no solution to repeat the old formulas. This would lead nowhere, and the effect would be repressive. But people are thinking about the Gospel and what it means today. We shall not be able to find a fresh expression of its meaning immediately, but it will come in words and deeds and in new orders. And this will occur as truly as the Gospel is not dead but alive, even today, the Gospel of the adoption of free sons. We should not be apprehensive of disputes, and, although we should not exaggerate, we should be willing to take risks. There is always danger in birth.

In this context I must say that I am not happy about some of our great fighters of the thirties having so readily denounced the slogan of "democratization" in the Church recently, their reason being the self-evident truth that in the Church the will of Christ, not the will of the people, is determinative. It is true, of course, that the will of Christ is determinative but that same will of Christ wants God's children to be of age, not kept in tutelage, and this implies the necessity in the Church of a democratic control and balance of power.

Our third question was: *Do you have this maturity once and for all?* Having stressed the unconditional granting and acknowledging of maturity as its prerequisite, we must now point out the dangers which threaten the maturity of each person and each group, and all the more so when maturity has been achieved. It is endangered from without and within by power politics and ideologies. Unfortunately, man himself is its greatest enemy.

The leaders of the Enlightenment and champions of a democracy come of age were by no means all optimists. The fundamental principle of democracy (which is so often mistakenly described as the principle of majority decision)—the principle of the permanent restriction and change of government—grew out of their concern for man's maturity and was partly based on the old-fashioned concept of "original sin." Surely it is a difficult task for our parties to preserve this spirit of democracy and the maturity of their members. But the dangers which are present here do not arise from the traditional conditions of power. The dangers of sinking back into tutelage are brought about by the modern necessities of life, for example, the monopoly of information and the role of the expert.

He who is directed by a cunning psychology is being stupefied, and he who is stupid is not of age. Monopolies of information in states, churches, parties, in economy and society today represent the most dangerous threat to maturity. He who is informed is superior to others and he wants to safeguard this state of superiority for himself. He needs the whole gamut of information from the daily to the weekly paper and to the expensive and exclusive journals issued by different organizations or obscure agencies. Even if something like "pure news" does exist, we may still be made victims of their selection, placing, and distribution. Control of information is the one means by which men are kept docile and willing to remain dependent. Hence the unpleasant struggle about radio, TV, newspaper cartels, and their owners must not cease.

A similar case is the expert knowledge so highly praised and probably indispensable today. Not everybody can have it. Who would not wish for the man with the most expert knowledge to be at the head of affairs? Thus, we reason that we expect the minister to take the chair in the meetings of his congregation, or the professor to have the power of decision in the university. Unfortunately, however, the expert is neither always objective nor immune to the temptation to bring his superiority into play in order to corroborate the dependence of others even more firmly. Modern students have found this out and now ridicule the expert. What else can they do to defend themselves? The expert is the magician of our time. An expert that does not encourage criticism, information which suppresses counterinformation—these are the modern idols which enslave their worshippers the same way as priests and magicians did in bygone times. Here we must be on our guard and not shun the cost of fighting the efforts to force people into the state of tutelage which we meet daily and in every walk of life.

Christian Maturity

Finally, we asked: *What do we mean by Christian maturity?* I am not going back on what I said about maturity being a human right for everybody, nor that it is to be granted to everybody one day, nor that in all stages of life, even in the Church, it is constantly threatened. Maturity is the most human of man's goods. There is really no "extra" given in Christian maturity, and even if there were it could not rest content with keeping it for itself. Thus, to speak of "Christian" maturity rouses suspicion.

Nevertheless, Christian maturity does relate to a guarantor. For us there exists a maturity defined and secured by Christ. We are not chasing after a phantom out of a total lack of commitment—as if such existed. Such phantoms exist only in systems of thought, in an illusion of logical absolutism where autonomy and heteronomy exclude each other, where self-destruction does not suffer any outside relationship. In reality, nobody has ever had an independent opinion without forming a viewpoint from the various relationships around him. No judgment of one's own has ever been made without resting on some bases. There is no judgment which is independent of some viewpoint, and for us Christ is a very strong viewpoint. In relation to him we are able to experience our independent coming of age.

One might ask, why should man's self-determination be curtailed by dealing with Christ? Why should our being of age be restricted by a prayerful relation to what is other than ourselves? However, it is actually the other way around. The Other, Christ, does not obstruct and lessen maturity. He stresses it and lifts it to a high rank. Nobody lives, thinks, and acts without taking his orientation from outside. Nobody does without any guarantors. *This* guarantor, however, is not interested in slavish obedience; he is interested in the relationship of love with a free partner.

It is delusion to think that breaking loose from Christ has given us independence. It has either made men lonely or ridiculously dependent on what everybody is doing. Now if someone lives on the strength of a different relationship we may compete with him gaily and calmly. Everywhere the apparently quite unrelated maturity soon degenerates into a worse immaturity, and one needs a strong grounding nowadays not to succumb to any cheap offer, not to let oneself be manipulated by the trend of psychological propaganda. Unfortunately, the lack of faith is no guarantee of reason and humanity. Freedom is costly.

However, we are really speaking here of maturity and not merely of "freedom." Freedom has a magnificent history with us in Germany, even in the Lutheran church. But it has frequently deteriorated to unlimited licentiousness and frequently produced the greatest lack of freedom. Ideals of freedom have often destroyed the rightful barriers between men and ended up in disrespect to the thought of others. The man come of age, however, cannot really cherish any ideals at the expense of the maturity of others. He does not impose any "views," as Mitscherlich says, but waits for "insights." Leaving the boundless state of dreams of his youth, he recognizes his limitations. His qualities are self-correction, self-criticism, reserve, and tolerance. By recognizing his dependences and his possibilities, he is set free. He knows that with his whole person he has to stand up for what he says. Maturity, or being of age, in the last instance, owes itself to that Other who allowed his mouth to be closed so that his maturity and ours might not be betrayed, who became entirely powerless so that others might regain power over themselves.

Bibliography of the Works of
Ronald Gregor Smith

Compiled by
Eugene Thomas Long

I. Books

Still Point. [Pseud. Ronald Maxwell.] London: Nisbet, 1943.

Back From the Front. [Pseud. Sam Browne.] London: Oliver and Boyd, 1946.

The New Man. New York: Harper, and London: S.C.M. Press, 1956. (The Alexander Love Lectures, given at Ormond College, Melbourne, 1955.)

. G. Hamann, 1730–1788: A Study in Christian Existence. London: Collins, and New York: Harper, 1960. (An enlarged version of the F. D. Maurice Lectures delivered at King's College, London, 1958.)

Secular Christianity. London: Collins, and New York: Harper, 1966. (Lectures delivered at McCormick Theological Seminary, Chicago, September 1964–January 1965.)

Martin Buber. London: Cary Kingsgate Press, and Richmond: John Knox, 1966. Swedish translation by Margareta Edgardh. Stockholm: A. B. Tryckmans, 1969.

The Free Man. London: Collins, 1969. Published in Philadelphia by the Westminster Press under the title *The Whole Man.*

The Doctrine of God. London: Collins, and Philadelphia: Westminster, 1970. (These are the lectures which Gregor Smith was to have delivered at Princeton Theological Seminary in 1969. From

the partially completed manuscript and notes which he left, the
were reconstructed and published by Käthe Gregor Smith and
A. D. Galloway as the Warfield Lectures for 1969.)

II. Books Edited and Translated

Buber, Martin. *I and Thou*. Translated by R. Gregor Smith. Edin
burgh: T. and T. Clark, 1937. Second Edition, with a postscrip
by the author added. New York: Scribners, 1958.

Barth, Karl. *The Germans and Ourselves*. Authorized translation by
R. Gregor Smith, with an Introduction by A. R. Vidler. London
Nisbet, 1945.

—————. *The Only Way*. Translated by R. Gregor Smith. New
York: Philosophical Library, 1947.

Smith, R. Gregor, ed. *Scottish Periodical* (1947–48). Ed. Edin
burgh, 1947–48.

Buber, Martin. *Between Man and Man*. Edited and translated b
R. G. Smith. London: Routledge, and New York: Macmillan
1948. Paperback edition with a new Introduction by R. Grego
Smith. London: Collins, 1961.

Jaspers, Karl. *The European Spirit*. Translated with an Introduction
by R. Gregor Smith. London: S.C.M. Press, 1948. Published with
an "Editional" in *Scottish Periodical* I (Summer 1948).

Smith, R. Gregor, ed. *The Enduring Gospel*. London: S.C.M. Press
1950.

Cori, Egon Caesar Conte. *The Destruction and Resurrection o
Pompeii and Herculaneum*. Translated by R. Gregor Smith and
Käthe Gregor Smith. London: Routledge, 1951.

Eichrodt, Walter. *Man in the Old Testament*. Translated b
R. Gregor Smith. London: S.C.M. Press, 1951.

Buber, Martin. *Right and Wrong*. Translated by R. Gregor Smith
London: S.C.M. Press, 1952.

Kramp, Willy. *The Prophecy*. Translated by R. Gregor Smith and
Käthe Gregor Smith. London: S. C. M. Press, 1952.

Barth, Karl. *Against the Stream*. Translated by R. Gregor Smith
London: S.C.M. Press, 1954.

Stauffer, Ethelbert. *Christ and the Caesars.* Translated by R. Gregor Smith and Käthe Gregor Smith. London: S.C.M. Press, 1955.

Ebeling, Gerhard. *The Nature of Faith.* Translated by R. Gregor Smith. Philadelphia: Muhlenberg Press, and London: Collins, 1961.

Bonhoeffer, Dietrich. *The Communion of Saints.* Translated by R. Gregor Smith. New York: Harper, 1963. Published in London by Collins under the title *Sanctorum Communio.*

Kierkegaard, Søren. *The Last Years.* Edited and translated with an Introduction by R. Gregor Smith. New York: Harper, and London: Collins, 1965.

Buber, Martin. *The Knowledge of Man.* Edited by Maurice Friedman, translated by M. Friedman and R. Gregor Smith. London: Allen and Unwin, 1965, New York: Harper, 1966.

Zimmermann, Wolf-Dieter. *I Knew Dietrich Bonhoeffer.* Edited by R. Gregor Smith with Wolf-Dieter Zimmermann, translated by Käthe Gregor Smith. New York: Harper, and London: Collins, 1966.

Smith, R. Gregor. Introduction to *World Come of Age,* edited by R. Gregor Smith. Philadelphia: Fortress Press, and London: Collins, 1967.

III. Articles

"D. H. Lawrence." In *Essays in Literature,* edited by John Murray. Published for the University of Edinburgh English Literature Society. Edinburgh: Oliver and Boyd, 1936.

"The Church as a Sign Upon the Earth. Its Peril and Goal." *The British Weekly* (October 16, 1941):25.

"God the Creator." *The British Weekly* (December 1941):151.

"Words." *Theology* (April 1942):220–227.

"What Christ Shows Us Of God." *The British Weekly* (April 9, 1942):15.

"The Canonical Evidence for the Doctrine of God the Creator." *Evangelical Quarterly* (April 1942):88–94.

"The Nineteenth Psalm: Nature and Grace." *The British Weekly* (November 26, 1942):101.

"The Minister in the Home Guard." *The British Weekly* (June 25, 1942):148.

"Must Preaching Be Interesting?" *The British Weekly* (July 23, 1942):190.

"Retribution and Mercy Are One in God." *Hibbert Journal* 40 (July 1942):326–330.

"Studies in Texts: Matthew V, 48." *Theology* 45 (August 1942): 93–95.

"Augustine and Donne: A Study in Conversion." *Theology* 45 (September 1942):147–159.

"Supplement on Nicodemus' Midnight Hour." *Christian News Letter* (October 1942). The journal *Frontier* is the lineal descendent of the *Christian News Letter*.

"The Church and the Churches." *Evangelical Quarterly* 15 (January 1943):32–39.

"Tertullian and Montanism." *Theology* 46 (June 1943):127–136.

"Theology in Scotland." *The British Weekly* (July 29, 1943):209.

"The Kingdom of God To-Day." *Evangelical Quarterly* 15 (October 1943):269–278.

"The Living and Speaking God." *Hibbert Journal* 42 (April 1944): 198–203.

"What Is Real Life?" *Theology* 47 (September 1944):203–206.

"Mr. Eliot's 'The Family Reunion' in the Light of Martin Buber's 'I and Thou'." *Theology* 50 (February 1947):59–64.

"T. S. Eliot's Späte Dichtung." *Bonner Universitätszeitung* 2 (July 1947):3.

"A Warning About Kierkegaard." *Scottish Periodical* (Summer 1948):80–83. *Scottish Periodical,* which was edited by R. Gregor Smith and published by Oliver and Boyd, Edinburgh, ceased to be published after the second volume in 1948. The first volume (Summer 1947) contained Gregor Smith's translation of an article by Rudolf Bultmann, "To Love Your Neighbor."

"The Thought of Martin Buber." *Burning Glass Paper* 18 (Kent: 1950).

"Karl Jaspers on Theology and Philosophy." *Hibbert Journal* 49 (October 1950):62–66.

"George McLeod and the Church of Scotland." *Frontier* (January 1950):99–104.

Buber, Martin. "Distance and Relation." Translated by R. Gregor Smith. *Hibbert Journal* 49 (January 1951):105–113. Reprinted in *Psychiatry* 20 (May 1957) and Buber's *The Knowledge of Man*. Edited by Maurice Friedman. New York: Harper and Row, 1965.

"Kierkegaard's Library." *Hibbert Journal* 50 (October 1951):18–21.

"An Exchange of Notes on T. S. Eliot. A Critique." *Theology Today* 7 (January 1951):503–506.

"The Essence of Protestantism." *The Listener* (January 24, 1952): 142–143.

"Danish Pastoral." *The British Weekly* (July 10, 1952).

"Evangelism by Persons." *The Student Movement* (October 1952): 17–20.

"Some Implications of Demythologising." *The Listener* (February 12, 1953):259–260.

"What Is Demythologizing?" *Theology Today* 10 (April 1953): 33–44.

"A Publisher Abroad." Four articles published in *The British Weekly* (June 18 and 25 and July 2 and 16, 1953).

"On Being Alone and Aldous Huxley." *The British Weekly* (April 15, 1954).

"The Christian and His Reading." *The British Weekly* (April 29, 1954):1.

"The Church and the World." *Student World* (Spring 1954).

"Germany Revisited." Four articles published in *The British Weekly* (July 1, 8, 15, and 22, 1954).

" 'Montanus' Introduces Himself." *The British Weekly* (February 4, 1954).

" 'Montanus' Asks: Do Your Old Sermons Keep You Humble?" *The British Weekly* (March 18, 1954).

"History and Self-understanding." *Theology Today* 11 (October 1954):335–341.

"Was Ist Entmythologisierung?" *Kerygma und Mythos* 4 (Hamburg: 1955):75–83.

"A Diary of Six Days in a Divided City." *The British Weekly* (January 27, 1955):7.

"Demythologising." *The Ecumenical Review* 7 (January 1955): 190–193.

"Is Christianity Intelligible?" *Theology* 58 (April 1955): 124–128.

"The Religion of Martin Buber." *Theology Today* 12 (July 1955): 206–215.

"University Life in East Germany. *The Australian Intercollegian* (August 1955).

"How Does the Christian Know?" *Religion in Education* (Autumn 1955).

"True Conversation." *Common Ground* 9 (September–October, 1955):7–12.

"Jesus Is Three Kings." *The Australian Intercollegian* (October 1955).

"The Character of Belief." *The Listener* 54 (November 10, 1955): 797–799.

Smith, R. Gregor. General Introduction to *An Existentialist Theology* by John Macquarrie. London: S.C.M. Press, 1955. (The "Library of Philosophy and Theology" had its beginning under the general editorship of Gregor Smith and this appears in several of the earlier volumes.)

"The Meaning of the Resurrection." *The Ecumenical Review* 4 (October 1956):91–94.

Smith, R. Gregor, and Rieger, J., eds. *The Bridge*. German-British Christian Fellowship: 1956.

"Christianity—Not Religion." *The Listener* 57 (March 28, 1957): 499–500.

"Man's Coming of Age." *The Listener* 57 (April 4, 1957): 549–550.

"Man's Encounter with God." *The Listener* 57 (April 11, 1957): 600–601.

"Is Christianity Still Relevant?" *The Listener* 57 (April 18, 1957): 633–634.

Buber, Martin. "Elements of the Interhuman." Translated by R. Gregor Smith. *Psychiatry* 20 (May 1957). Reprinted in Buber's *The Knowledge of Man*. New York: Harper, 1965.

"University Sermon." *The Cambridge Review* 79 (February 15, 1958):351–355.

Smith, R. Gregor, and Henderson, Ian. "Schottland," and "Theologiegeschichte des 19/20 Jh. S, in Schottland." *Evangelisches Kirchenlexicon* 3 (Gottingen: Vandenhoeck and Ruprecht, 1959): 842–846, 1397–1401.

"The Disappearing God: A Discussion Between J. P. Corbett, an Agnostic and R. Gregor Smith, a Christian." *The Listener* (January 21, 1960):127–129.

'A Theological Perspective of the Secular." *The Christian Scholar* 43 (March 1960):11–23.

'The Hamann Renaissance." *The Christian Century* 77 (June 29, 1960):768–769.

'Church, State and Freedom. Can 1960 Learn from 1560?" *The Manchester Guardian* (August 11, 1960).

'The Nature of Faith." *Sermons to Intellectuals*, edited by Franklin H. Littell. New York: Macmillan, 1963.

'Hamann and Kierkegaard." In *Zeit und Geschichte: Dankesgabe an Rudolf Bultmann zum 80 Geburtstag*, edited by Erich Dinkler. Tubingen: J.C.B. Mohr (1964) and *Kierkegaardiana* 5 (1964).

'The Crisis About God." *Crux* 4 (1965).

"Martin Buber," "Dietrich Bonhoeffer," "Søren Aabye Kierkegaard," "Enlightenment," "Johann Georg Hamann," and "Worldliness." In *Dictionary of Christian Ethics*, edited by John Macquarrie. London: S.C.M. Press, and New York: Harper, 1965: 36–37; 33–34; 188–89; 105; 144; 363–64.

'Post-Renaissance Man." In *Conflicting Images of Man*, edited by W. Nicholls. New York: Seabury Press, 1966, pp. 31–49. An excerpt appears in *Breakthrough* 14:11–16.

'Bonhoeffer 21 Years After." *The Methodist Recorder* (April 7, 1966):1.

"Resurrection and Faith." *New Christian* (April 7, 1966). This journal merged with *The Christian Century* in June 1970.

"Christlicher Glaube und Sakularismus." *Zeitschrift für Theologie und Kirche* 63 (May 1966):33–48.

"Martin Buber's View of the Interhuman." *The Jewish Journal o* *Sociology* 8 (June 1966):64–80.

" 'The New Morality?' An Introduction," and "Summing Up." *Breakthrough* 15:3–6 and 36–39. (Symposium at Universit Teachers' Group Conference, St. Anne's College, Oxford, 1966)

"Technology and Ethics: A Theological Comment." *Contact* (Ma 1968):26–29.

"The Meaning of Secular Theology." *Venture Magazine* (Glasgow June 1968).

"J. G. Hamann and the Princess Gallitzin: An Ecumenical En counter." In *Philomathes: Studies and Essays in the Humanitie in Memory of Philip Merlan,* edited by Robert B. Palmer anc Robert Hamerton-Kelly. The Hague: Martinus Nijhoff, 1971 330–340.

IV. *Selected Essays from Unpublished Manuscripts* *University of Glasgow Library*

"Humanism and Faith: With Constant Reference to the Life anc Work of Søren Kierkegaard." Written in Denmark about 1938

"The Thought of Martin Buber." B.B.C. Third Program Broadcast March 30, 1949.

"Demythologising." Revision of an address delivered at several uni versities in North America in 1952, including Boston University Bethany College, Chicago; McMaster College, Hamilton, On tario; and Knox College, Toronto.

"God in Eclipse." B.B.C. Third Program Broadcast, April 1953.

"The Way of Wisdom." B.B.C. Third Program Broadcast, Febru ary 1956.

"The Doctrine of Atonement" and "Apologetics." Lectures in Syste matic Theology at Glasgow University, 1957.

"Vocation or Calling." Lectures in Systematic Theology at Glasgow University, 1958.

"Johann Georg Hamann, Christian Existentialist." Presidential Ad dress to the Edinburgh University Theological Society, December 24, 1958.

"The Background of the New Man" and "The Gospel for the New

Man." Addresses delivered at a S.C.M. Theological Conference, April 1959.

"The Nature of Christian Action." Lectures in Systematic Theology at Glasgow University, October 1959.

"Faith and Power. An address for the Iona Community, Scotland, November 1960.

"Jesus Christ and Modern Theology." Two addresses delivered at a Postgraduate Refresher Course, Dunblane, Scotland, May 13, 1964. Mimeographed.

"Is the Resurrection a Historical Fact?" and "Faith." Lectures probably written at McCormick Seminary in 1964.

"Dietrich Bonhoeffer." An address delivered at Southern Methodist University, Dallas, Texas, December 4, 1964.

"Christian Faith and Secularism." Written October 1965. Appears to be a revision of a paper read at Randolph-Macon College, Ashland, Va., in 1964.

"An Introduction to Theology." Lectures in Systematic Theology delivered at Glasgow University, 1966–67.

"Church of Scotland: Our Understanding of the Bible as the Word of God." An address for the Church of Scotland–Scandinavian Churches Conference held at Nordfjordeid, Norway, August 1968.

Index

God, Secularization, and History

COMPOSED IN LINOTYPE ELECTRA BY HERITAGE PRINTERS
WITH SELECTED LINES OF DISPLAY IN PERPETUA.
PRINTED LETTERPRESS BY HERITAGE PRINTERS ON
WARREN'S UNIVERSITY TEXT, AN ACID-FREE PAPER
WATERMARKED WITH THE
UNIVERSITY OF SOUTH CAROLINA PRESS COLOPHON.
BINDING BY KINGSPORT PRESS
IN HOLLISTON'S ROXITE.